LINA IN SEARCH OF LINA

The History and Treatment of a Patient with Multiple Personality Disorder

Rolando I. Haddad, M.D.

Chicago Spectrum Press
Louisville, Kentucky 40207

Chicago Spectrum Press
4824 Brownsboro Center
Louisville, Kentucky 40207
502-899-1919

Printed in the U.S.A.

10 9 8 7 6 5 4 3 2 1

ISBN: 1-58374-095-3

Cover design and book illustration by Sandy Price

ACKNOWLEDGMENTS

I'm grateful to my wife, Elsa. Without her encouragement, the writing of this book might not have occurred. She holds a Ph.D. in art and literature and has had courses in psychology as well. She was a teacher in Cuba, but her full-time job has been to be my wife, my advisor, and my support. She is the wonderful mother of our three great children, and in my private practice, she became my office manager. She is a woman with a heart full of compassion and tenderness. She was well aware of Lina's progression in therapy and all of the suffering Lina was going through. Many times going back home from the office, she would ask me the name of the Alter (alternate personality) who came in that day, for if she was around when Lina arrived or left the office, my wife was able to detect changes in her personality.

I am grateful to Pedro Portes, Ph.D., Professor of Psychology at the University of Louisville, for reviewing this book, and for his commentaries and guidance on how to make this book a reality.

I am grateful to my daughter, Gloria H. Taggett, Ph.D. in clinical psychology. She gave me valuable and up-to-date information which helped me with this book.

I have to thank Dorothy Kavka who helped me edit this manuscript.

And also, thank you, Mr. Wise One.

CONTENTS

PREFACE

The author recounts one of his most challenging and complex cases in ways that serve the curious reader. Although the book is written much like a detective novel, at the same time, it offers an expert resource for those who study and teach psychology and psychiatry. At one level, the Story of Lina shows how a multiple personality disorder is socially constructed under conditions of stress, as many other forms of psychopathology. It helps us understand the role of early, disturbed relationships, self-esteem and subsequent adult reactions and well being. At another level, for the professional reader, it offers new insights in diagnosis, treatment and perhaps another important data point for researchers in this field. How the patient's own courageous efforts to help herself in response to her doctor's persistent and strategic interventions tells a story of how humanity and expert support can transform a clinical condition.

Several other books have been written already on this uncanny illness. Some have been contested as cases that actually meet the criteria for proper diagnosis. I would venture to note Dr. Haddad's book is unique in its own right, and most definitely qualifies as the best treatise on Multiple Personality Disorder, told in the most humane and professional manner. The author is a scientist as well as an expert clinician. I am most pleased to write this preface in that I can point out how his own life experiences, which have included not only vast clinical experience, but also painful and distressful experiences, have contributed to the unique contributions in this work. To be more direct, I would argue that perhaps what others have missed in the past insofar as understanding and actually resolving this complex personality disorder may be in part a function of the interaction between a well prepared mind and shattering experiences . The latter, which are worth an autobiography on their own right, may be considered instrumental in having allowed the synthesis presented in this book. Having first hand knowledge about conditions that can shatter the human psyche, and having the capacity to avoid its psychopathological consequences may be one reason why this book stands alone in uncovering the dynamics of what can fragment a human personality.

It may be useful to point to several important differences between this likely classic in the field and some of its better known predecessors. The rather well publicized predecessors that eventually gained international attention through film; *Three Faces of Eve, Sybil* and others, merit a brief acknowledgment and offer a baseline from which to assay the merit of this work

In sum, this book, while written to extend the understanding of the lay public and those families with similar although rare cases, is also ideal for courses in psychopathology and the training of mental health professionals. Rarely has a case study offered as much insight into the making of personality disorder, and particularly this particular form of a "split" personality. How the case of Lina deviates from other schizoid, schizophrenic variations is didactic in nature. The student as well as expert of psychopathology will walk away from reading this book enriched in understanding. This reader will be able to reflect and to surely become more effective in treating such cases. But more importantly, he will be able to understand the making of borderline, transient states that approximate the disorder. He is more likely to understand how certain distressful, abusive conditions can interact with personality to produce this and other forms of disassociation that are more subtle. The role of gender is implicit in the author's analysis, again providing an important cue about environmental determinants for various disorders.

Finally, the reintegration of Lina as a functional, competent human being is priceless. The carefully documented sequence of events offers a map to those who may in the future encounter similar cases and its variants. The author's vast knowledge in this area is presented humbly yet provides a standard for clinical effectiveness. While I would not doubt that this book may be sensationalized into yet another film, it is clear that its merit will remain intact in guiding those genuinely concerned about the tearing and rebuilding of human psychological competence.

–Pedro R. Portes, Ph.D.

ABOUT MULTIPLE PERSONALITY DISORDER

Multiple Personality Disorder (MPD) is a dissociative disorder characterized by disruptions of identity, feelings, and memory. It has been described as two or more personalities surfacing or demonstrating themselves in one person, possessing distinctive characteristics and *individuality*. The body performs and behaves in accordance with the personality showing at the time, and the patient is unable to recall personal information that cannot be explained by ordinary forgetfulness.

The disturbance is not due to direct psychological effects of a drug or any substance (e. g., blackouts or chaotic behavior during alcohol intoxication) or a general medical condition (e. g., partial seizure disorder).

In 1994, the term Multiple Personality Disorder was changed to "Dissociative Identity Disorder." I will briefly explain the meaning of some words used frequently in this book.

Personality is an entity who is within the person suffering from MPD. When this person is confronted with some specific (and other times not so specific) stressful situations, this entity (or personality) emerges and becomes evident, taking over the person's usual and daily performance. This may last for a brief period of time, i.e., minutes, hours, or up to a few days. Usually, there is more than one "personality" or entity (also called "Alters"), and they represent different aspects of the emotions and performance of a human being, such as anger, wisdom, shyness, aggressiveness, sexuality, etc. Recently, a newspaper reported a psychiatrist uncovering around two hundred personalities in one single patient. Physicians and counselors with experience may report cases with seven or less more basic, different personalities. If many more are detected or showing, they could be what is known as fragmentation or splitting personalities.

Fragmentation or Split refers to a portion of an entity or personality. They may have many years of existence. They are created by the subconscious in order to express a limited range of emotions that the host may feel uncomfortable with expressing consciously.

Host Personality or "Executive Control" is the entity that is in control of the mind and the body at the time the change occurs

Alter (or Alternate Personality) is any personality or fragment other than the host.

Integration is the fusion of different Alters into fewer entities or personalities. Integration occurs when the host is in full control of ideas, emotions or decisions. It has been reported that even when treatment is successful, some Alters remain and although they lack full control, they are still able to emerge briefly during times of crisis.

Core is the name we use in Lina's case to refer to the *Original Personality*. In text books, the *Original Personality* is described as the personality developed first in life.

Switching is the showing or fluctuation of different existing Alters and their manifestation in the host.

SOME HISTORY ABOUT MPD

Before Robert Louis Stevenson published his book, *Jekyll and Hyde*, in 1886 portraying what is considered a double personality, Dr. Mitchell from the University of Pennsylvania wrote about the first recorded multiple personality in 1811.

In 1905, *The Dissociation of a Personality* was published by Morton Prince. "Eve, A Case of Multiple Personality" was reported in 1954 in the *Journal of Abnormal Psychology.* Finally, in 1970, Dr. Cornelia Wilber, a psychiatrist in Lexington, Kentucky, reported the treatment of *Sybil*, a case of MPD.

Other books on the subject include *Lost in the Mirror,* by Moskovitz; *Gemme du Monde*, by Schreiber; and *Madonna de las Siete Lunas* (Spanish).

So, as we can see, the concept of MPD is not new, but new data regarding this disorder started flourishing by 1980. The reality of MPD has been abused and distorted by television and movies producers, and even the diagnosis of MPD has been abused by some psychiatrists. When I first learned about Lina's diagnosis from local qualified professionals who employed standard psychological tests, I began doing research and read several books recommended to me about this disorder. I wanted to be sure, as much as I could, to "not do harm" by using an unorthodox approach. The books I found very useful included, *Disorder of Self,* by J.F. Masterson, M.D., and *Treatment of Multiple Personality Disorder*, by B. G. Braun, M.D.

NAME OF PERSONALITIES, ALTERS AND SPLITS IN LINA'S CASE

The first alter I encountered was *Lynny Sue*. She was around six years old and manifested herself a few times, mainly at the beginning of the therapy. She mentioned *Lizzy*, who was four years old, but Lizzy never came to the surface. It seems that Lizzy was the first to suffer the sexual trauma. *Lonnie* was a five year old child mentioned a couple of times.

In total, *seven children* without given names were mentioned; they never took part in Lina's therapy.

The *She* was one of the oldest Alters. She represented the need for punishment and self-destruction, and was full of guilt and shame. By the end of therapy, the She faded away and was not a threat for self-destructive behavior, such as suicidal ideations and self-mutilation.

The *No One* was one of the oldest and most powerful Alters and was a masculine figure. He displayed his power from the beginning of therapy until the end. He had aggressive, destructive and homicidal tendencies from his creation up to the first few months of commencing therapy. The name of No One was self-adopted in order to avoid responding to any questions; instead he would answer, "Don't know," or "Don't want to know."

The *Tank* was created in the host's early teens and was present after the children "disappeared." I came to believe that he could be the root of the No One.

The *Angry One* was a split of the No One, created in order to manifest strong, angry statements without the destructive tendencies of the No One. This Alter faded away after the No One became "civil" (as he described himself by mid-therapy).

The *Male Guardian* was reported to be the most powerful figure, and Lina was able to give a very good description of him. I refer to him as a "figure" because I have no recollection of him manifested as an Alter or Personality during my many hours in therapy with Lina. He was mentioned many times and was described to me as the entity that could control the No One, but when both of them united, the force of their union could be devastating.

The *Female Guardian* was mentioned many times as a soft, yet firm figure. She also never established direct contact with me.

The *Gentle One* was an angelic figure, sweet, soft, easygoing, who existed briefly, only to disappear, unable to deal with so much suffering endured by the host. She manifested herself to me only once, but did not speak during that brief encounter. I detected her presence by an aura of gentleness, peace, and light that emanated momentarily over Lina's face. Shortly thereafter, someone named the *Feeler* and another named the *Explorer* were sent to the surface by an unknown figure, but they quickly vanished, leaving no trace for the rest of the treatment.

The *Shell* took over when the Gentle One disappeared. She was an entity with no emotions, no show of pain or anger. She was described as a flat personality, with an "I don't care" attitude. To the best of my memory and after reviewing my notes, I do not remember having any significant encounters with her, although that name was mentioned several times throughout the course of therapy by Lina and the Wise One.

Veronica was mentioned a few times and reported as a reliable, hard-working, skillful woman, but I had no interaction at all with her.

The nagging *Bitch,* the elegant *Lady* and the sexy *Woman,* I feel strongly were split of a personality, that I could not clearly identify. They manifested themselves to me a couple of times and were accepted as Alters. The Bitch was, at times, confused, resembling in lesser degree, the Angry One. I do not remember having any direct confrontation with her, but Lina's husband complained very frequently about his wife's "bitchy attitude." The Lady was skillful at shopping, combining colors, make-up, dress, and good manners. Several weeks before the treatment ended, the Lady and Lina became more and more integrated. I saw the Woman one afternoon. She stayed over one hour, and it was the only time she came to the surface. I presume that by the end of treatment the Shell, the Bitch, the Woman, and the Lady became integrated into the Core, each one of them with more realistic and, at the same time, milder attidudes. The She and Lynny Sue were also included in this integration, but with a much lower profile.

The *Core* refers to the basic personality that Lina was born with, but was set aside and opaqued very early in her childhood by those other Personalities.

The *Gate Keeper* controls the incoming and outgoing flow of information. He was in charge of the amount and intensity of "memories" allowed to filter through the wall and be remembered by Lina. This name was mentioned by the Wise One and Lina often, but I never established any type of communication nor could I get a clear profile of this alter. The Gate Keeper could be a combination of the Male and the Female Guardian, or he/she could be one of the *Protectors*.

The name *Caretaker* is frequently mentioned without a definite entity appearing.

The *Teen* preceded *Lonnie*, who was described as a tomboy. They both disappeared when *Rowdy* emerged. Rowdy was irresponsible, a wild, happy, hedonistic, unruly personality. She got in trouble a lot and she was the one who was present when Lina became pregnant for the first time.

The *Wise One* never revealed his age. When asked about events that happened in the early years of Lina's life, this nice, soft-spoken personality would manage to send me some other Alter. He sent Lynny Sue. He was careful not to antagonize the No One openly, but he managed to be close to the Guardians. He gave wise guidance and valuable information. When I asked Lina to write whatever came to her mind (in between sessions of therapy), the Wise One did most of the writing.

A diagram at the end of the book shows the sequence of events and the appearance of different personalities in Lina's life.

ABOUT THE BOOK

This is the story of a patient who developed MPD (Multiple Personality Disorder) as a consequence of traumatic events she experienced in the early years of her life. It is her story from infancy to adulthood and the story of her family. It tries to describe the way her subconscious reacted and protected her from "aggressive happenings" in her life. Her reaction was not the result of a psychosis. Maybe it was "crazy," what happened to her. Some would call it a sick mind or a fantasy, but for Lina, it was a sad reality.

Besides repetitive sexual abuse very early in her childhood, many other traumatic events happened at different times. She grew up in a very dysfunctional family. This book will try to show the way a sensitive person reacted to escape from so much guilt, shame, fear and horror that were piling up in her life. It also reflects on all the misfortune that this reaction brought to her and the people around her.

The idea to publish this book came little by little by reading and analyzing notes I asked Lina to write while in therapy. At first, she was not in favor of publishing this book. She did not want to end up in court pointing to those who sexually abused her. We checked with a lawyer, in order to give her reassurance that this was not going to happen. She finally gave me permission to go ahead; she fully cooperated and became involved in her recovery process with a positive attitude.

The book does not follow a detailed sequence and at times appears to be repetitive. I tried to combine the way that therapy was conducted, showing the progression of treatment, with Lina's history. However, names and places have been changed in order to protect her identity.

I do not pretend that this a text book, nor can I call myself an expert in treating MPD. This work only reflects my treatment approach in this case and its positive outcome and benefits.

As we will see later on, Lina was hospitalized many times and given countless amounts of psychotropic drugs by other physicians. I promised her that I would avoid such treatment as much as possible.

I also knew of other psychiatrists who were treating MPD patients with hypnosis and/or sodium amytal interviews in order to gather data and history in order to interpret actual events. Regressive hypnotherapy is a very useful tool in this kind of treatment, but it unlatches old traumatic memories leading to deeper distress and risking the possible emergence and development of a more complicated mechanism of defense of the subconscious. There were similar reactions with the sodium amytal interview, "truth" serum, which is injected slowly in the vein while asking key questions to the patient.

I also was aware of the use and abuse of physical restraints to control outbursts of rage or destructive behavior and the use of psychotropic drugs to modify or control emotions, thoughts, and behavior, and the frequent and extended hospitalization for "the need to protect and control the patient's destructive behavior."

I did not see a need for using any of these treatments with Lina. Maybe she was different or perhaps it was a matter of trust [positive transference].

In those years of treatment, I had to hospitalize her for four to five days, mainly for my own peace of mind, because she was having strong suicidal ideas at that time. A small dose of a mild tranquilizer was all she needed for the acute turmoil she was experiencing during those days. Those were the only medications and hospitalizations I prescribed.

There are, to the best of my knowledge, five books published regarding the treatment of patients with MPD, yet *Lina in Search of Lina* is different, if not unique, since my approach with Lina was more simplistic.

INTRODUCTION

Traumatic events in early life can provoke drastic changes in a human being. Those changes may become evident at any given time following the trauma(s), even years later. The mental and/or physical consequences are related to the intensity of the trauma, thc sensitivity or receptivity of the individual, previous traumatic events, and other factors.

In this book, I try to show the suffering and struggle of a person who was exposed in early life to severe emotional distress. We may imagine a brick wall around her, enclosing many unpleasant memories, darkness, and no real understanding of a sequence of events. "Guardians" protect the traumatic secrets from being remembered. In the patient's mind, those Guardians are powerful entities with a definite purpose – to protect her from further suffering and trauma. The memories are shut down to avoid remembering the pain. They are contained, and thus the suffering cannot be remembered. Yet, often, weird and painful feelings make her life miserable.

This book is not fiction. It is the story of a well-mannered patient named Lina, for whom deep-rooted traumatic events in her younger years drastically changed and distorted her life.

Those repressed memories surfaced at times to the conscious mind (more frequently at some times than at others), but without defined cognitive proprieties. They generated emotions of intense fear, anxiety, panic, or terror. They produced anger, outrage, aggressiveness, and chronic deep depression, with frequent feelings of self-destruction. In Lina's case, homicidal intent occurred at least once.

In her tormented mind, entities were created with different personalities. Those Personalities (or "Alters") were very well defined within Lina's mind. She heard different voices talking, quarreling, and fighting inside of her head, which caused her frequent severe headaches and vivid flashes of past events without sequence. Those Personalities were not only identified by different voices, but they were also manifested by Lina's different facial expressions, body movements, and actions. Often they were threatening and, at times, destructive.

All of this led Lina to have frequent psychiatric hospitalizations, prescriptions for psychotropic drugs, forced restraints, being locked into seclusion rooms, and police interventions for violent behavior. She could not control the outpouring of hate, pain, perplexity, and confusion.

Lina asked many times, "Oh God, why do the 'voices' tell me, I'm bad, I will burn in Hell, I need to be purified, I need to be punished? What did I do wrong? Who am I? Where am I coming from? Where am I going? I'm lost! Why this confusion, this anger? Why this feeling of emptiness surrounded by this intense darkness?"

Her story shows how powerful the mind is over the body and how early trauma can distort, mask, change, and deeply disrupt a life years later.

One of the basic lessons taught at medical school is, "First, do no harm." When I met Lina, I tried to send her to another psychiatrist who was more experienced in dealing with patients with MPD because I did not want to cause more damage to her psyche.

I did not have a guideline to follow, which is why I was not feeling confident as her therapist, but her husband insisted, "You or nobody else. If you do not want to try, we will go to no one."

An Alter in the form of a Guardian figure was created in Lina's mind to prevent painful memories from coming to the surface. This was one of her many Personalities, a powerful figure, as we will see later on. But the Guardian was not the only one aware of what was behind that Wall; there were other "Alters" or Personalities. In some instances, they are called the "Gate Keepers," who were there to prevent any more suffering, distress, or pain in Lina.

At the same time, however, the Alters fought for survival, control, and domination, and so by their performance, they provoked more distress and pain.

They called Lina weak and gutless. They used derogatory names. They wanted to make her as strong and capable as they were. They emotionally shielded her, but, at the same time, they were fighting for control and supremacy over her. They wanted to be independent, resenting ideas or even attempts of autonomy.

After much struggle, Lina accepted therapy and progressed without further damage to her psyche. She started to be in control of her emotions without the need to escape into "somebody else."

With therapy, the Wall started crumbling and light started coming through. Memories became clearer, or at least less foggy. Painful memories started matching painful feelings. Psychotherapy was gradually better accepted, and cooperation among the Alters began to occur. The healing process began.

After three plus years and over two hundred hours of psychotherapy, Lina ended her treatment.

CHAPTER ONE

HOW LINA BECAME MY PATIENT AND HOW I GOT INVOLVED

At the end of 1992, one of my patients asked me to see his wife. He described her as being unpredictable, with frequently changing moods, sometimes from one minute to the next. At first, I refused to see her on a one-on-one basis. I felt it would be more appropriate if she became involved in ongoing therapy with her husband, and I was unwilling to open a clinical chart for her alone, independent from her husband. For the last six years, he had been recovering from alcoholism, but for the last year, I had been treating him for recurrent chronic depression.

I met Allen (Lina's husband) in 1991, when he was hospitalized for severe depression and mood swings. I was his attending physician at the hospital, and upon his discharge, I continued providing him outpatient treatment in my office once a week. Then a couple of months later, his appointments were spaced out to every three to four weeks.

During his sessions, he would complain about the type of life he was having with his wife. Her problems appeared to be complicated. Descriptions he gave me regarding his wife's erratic, unpredictable behavior and her frequent mood swings made me extremely hesitant to be involved in her treatment. Finally, I agree to see her at least once for a first-hand evaluation, mostly to please her husband and to gain some idea of what was going on, or perhaps I was just curious.

The first day she came to my office, she appeared to be frightened. She was dressed in a less than fashionable manner and her hair was not well combed. She seemed curious, but distant, and somewhat guarded. She maintained poor eye contact with me and seemed to be paying more attention to the books on the shelf and the diplomas hanging on the wall. Finally, she sat on the edge of her chair, while at the same time, she pushed the chair away from the desk. Her husband tried to reassure her in a very soft manner, so soft I could detect some flare of caution. He tried to make a formal introduction. Her handshake was brief, timid, and tangential. I told her I appreciated her coming to see me, and after a while, I asked her what she thought was going on in her life.

She gave me a history of many years of fogginess and turmoil, with her head hurting almost constantly, and recent episodes of violent and destructive behavior, leading to police intervention and ending in a psychiatric hospitalization. She did not explain why or what triggered the incident. She was indeed confused. She said she had frequent suicidal thoughts and several suicide attempts which were followed by involuntary psychiatric hospitalizations. She had gone through countless psychiatric and counseling interventions and had been prescribed endless amounts of psychiatric drugs. She said she had had enough of these situations.

The brief history she gave helped me to understand her fearful, guarded frame of mind and the negative attitude she was showing.

She also mentioned voices inside of her head fighting. For years her husband had been complaining of her disappearing, at times for one or more days. When he would ask her where she had been, her answer was, "I don't know. I don't know. I don't know where I was; I don't know what happened." This all seemed similar to blackouts due to alcoholism, but alcohol dependency or alcohol addiction was not a tentative diagnosis in Lina's case.

Right then I started thinking of different diagnostic possibilities. She was acceptably organized and therefore could not be diagnosed as a possible schizophrenic. The voices she was describing were not similar to what I have heard from previous schizophrenic patients in my 20 plus years of practicing psychiatry. She was guarded, but not paranoid. In the spectrum of personality disorders, she could be classified as histrionic, or perhaps dissociated. Indeed, I was curious, but at that moment, a MPD diagnosis did not enter my mind.

There is an old saying in medicine — in order to make a diagnosis, we need to think in the disease. In the practice of medicine, different diagnostic possibilities need to be considered. If you don't know what you are dealing with, you cannot provide appropriate treatment. You can treat symptoms, but symptoms will continue changing and different medications for different symptoms could be prescribed over and over. In Lina's case, she had already been given many medications, targeting a broad spectrum of multiple and chronic complaints and symptoms.

In my medical practice, many times my first diagnostic impression was usually correct, and I was able to reach that impression through a brief interview. With Lina's case, I felt uneasy, not knowing what I was dealing with.

I requested a psychological testing with a qualified psychologist, and also asked Carol, one of my co-therapists, to interview Lina. Carol saw Lina in two or three sessions and was able to develop a positive transference with her. Carol told me that while interviewing her, Lina changed her voice and attitude.

"Someone with a voice like a very young child," said Carol, "identified herself as 'Lizzy.'" Yet, when the session was over, Lina did not remember this voice or what it said.

I received a report of the results of the psychological testing and from both ends came the same strong diagnostic impression: I was indeed dealing with a patient with MPD. According to *The Diagnostic Manual For Psychiatric Conditions (*DSM-IIIR), MPD is characterized as ". . . the person's identity is temporarily forgotten or gone and a new identity may be assumed or imposed." In the new DSM-IV of the American Psychiatric Association (APA), MPD is called "Dissociative Identity Disorder." After reading the criteria in order to make the proper diagnosis, I later found it to be a pale reflection of what I was to encounter in Lina's case.

At this point I was facing a challenging situation, unique for me. I couldn't remember having a case like this in my psychiatric experience. At that time I was also working at the Jefferson County Correctional Facility in Louisville, Kentucky, as Chief of the Mental Health Department. I was dealing with inmates who presented with a broad gamut of mental problems, besides the criminal or felony charges that brought them to jail. One of my co-workers there was a psychiatric registered nurse who had experience working with disturbed patients who had been exposed to rituals or satanic cults and who were allegedly abused in early life. He also claimed to have experience providing therapy for some of those patients who had developed MPD.

He was indeed good at working with and helping inmates who were emotionally disturbed, so I contracted with him to provide therapy for Lina, one and a half hours a week, every week, with a minimum of six months up to perhaps two years, if needed. My participation was to be passive, as an observer; as it turned out, therapy lasted for about three years, and I ended up being Lina's only therapist from the early stages of treatment.

My co-worker saw her for a month or so, until he had an encounter with some of the Alters. In one session, one Personality named the No One came to interact with him in a rather violent manner. The therapist then withdrew from the case and I found myself providing treatment for something for which I had no previous experience.

"We will not go to see anybody else," Lina and Allen told me when I tried to give them a referral to a psychiatrist who had experience dealing with MPD.

On December 9, 1992, when I saw Lina for the first time in order to take her clinical and psychiatric history, my first, tentative diagnostic impression was Major Depression, recurrent, with psychotic features and frequent suicidal ideations. I also thought that Bipolar Disorder might also be another diagnostic possibility. I left blank considerations of personality problems. Lina gave me permission to request clinical files from previous psychotherapies, counselings, and hospitalizations. The first available information was dated 6/17/1977. The diagnosis given at that time was "Depressive Neurosis," and therapy was terminated in June of 1979. That clinical file was closed in January 1980 and the prognosis given was "good."

She entered into therapy again on February 8, 1982 to March 4, 1982 and this time the diagnosis given was "Adjustment Disorder with mixed emotional features." Her chief complaints at that time were having problems falling to sleep, being apathetic, lying around, not wanting to get dressed, and crying spells.

In November 1982, she went into therapy again and the diagnosis given at that time was "Marital Problems." No other data was available until March 12, 1984, when she was seen by another therapist, who diagnosed: "1-Adjustment Disorder with Depressed Mood," "2-Parent-Child Problems," "3-ACOA" (adult children of alcoholic), and "4-Compulsive Personality."

She was hospitalized again from July 21, 1986 to August 5, 1986. This time she reported "hearing voices," among another symptoms. The discharge diagnosis was "Dysthymic Disorder," "Generalized Anxiety," and "Other Family Circumstances." In 1987, another set of diagnoses was given, "Dysthymic Disorder," "Generalized Anxiety Disorder," and "ACOA."

Lina had seven psychiatric hospitalizations and several more for medical-surgical services. She had a gastric bypass, an ovarian cyst removed, exploratory laparoscopy, a tubal ligation, a cholecystectomy, hypertension, a ganglion cyst removed from her left wrist, and a hysterectomy. On top of that, she had emotional crises: one in January 1973, two in 1978, one in July 1985, one in March 1986, one in December 1992, and one in February 1993, all requiring psychiatric intervention.

With that extensive history of medical intervention, her reluctance and fear of getting involved again in therapy was understandable. She was very distrustful of doctors and mental health professionals. I, myself, was not too enthusiastic with this type of therapeutic challenge.

By the time I took over the therapy, Lina's personalities were already evident. Each one had a character and strength. At times, Lina would show drastic changes in her voice and facial expression, and her attitude and gestures were sometimes threatening and almost belligerent. Once the Alter was "gone," Lina's voice was again soft, and her manner well-behaved; she would not have any recollection, knowledge, or memory of what had just happened to her.

The Alters were defending their individuality, struggling for independence, not autonomy. Their justification was "to protect her from painful memories."

At this time, I felt that I was involved in a group therapy setting, and not just dealing with Lina alone. It was indeed a very strange feeling and a new experience for me, talking and listening to different people who were within one person.

Early in therapy, one of the Alters mentioned the "Pig House" as a place that was very distressful for Lina. At that early level of therapy, Lina was not aware of the conversations between the Alters and the therapist.

Trying to bring some memories to the surface so we could learn about them and have some material to work with, I asked her what she could remember about the Pig House. Before this, she was relaxed, not showing any distress or turmoil, but as soon as I mentioned the "Pig House," her reaction showed how frightened she was and drastic changes happened in a fraction of a second. She appeared terrified, shaking so intensely that the chair she was sitting on became part of her body, dancing and jerking like a severe epileptic convulsion.

She was mumbling some words, uttering over and over, "No, No!," and then shouting at the top of her lungs. She also mentioned the "No Toe." This seemed to be a very odd name for an Alter. Indeed, he was not an Alter. At that moment I could only guess about this name, but down the road we learned that "No Toe" was a man who was missing one toe from his foot, and that he most probably frequently abused her sexually when she was a child.

When the crisis was over, my co-therapist and I felt like we were walking on the edge of a razor blade, so we did not ask Lina more questions.

The first few sessions with my co-therapist went very well. He was able to elicit data from Lina. I was there only as a passive participant. He knew what he was doing, but when he quit, I found myself dealing with a patient surrounded by a constellation of symptoms pointing in different directions and a marginal attitude of cooperation for therapy.

Again, I had to tell Lina and her husband about my lack of experience with her problem, but they refused to go to anybody else. Lina was slowly developing insight into her condition and showing some level of acceptance.

A paragraph taken from the psychological testing report reads, "The woman entered into treatment with Dr. H. because her husband's treatment has been successful with this physician.

She was becoming more upset by the recent intensification of her symptoms and believed Dr. H. to be trustworthy. Lina does continue a regular dialog with the voices in her head, which she is accepting to be different parts of herself."

Early in therapy, Lina mentioned some names given to some of those voices. The youngest one belonged to a four year old named Lizzy, who appeared early in the evaluation done by Carol. Another voice, soft-spoken, deep, and well-mannered, belonged to the Wise One, who appeared to be very eager to cooperate and advise, and who intervened often. As therapy progressed, I learned to respect and listen to this Alter. His concern was to avoid doing more harm and to protect The Core.

He was different from the other two Alters: The Angry One and the No One. These two were very powerful. They were threatening, loud, imposing, demanding, and aggressive. At that time, I considered them to be potentially destructive. They had the same goal as the other Alters — to protect the Core — but their approaches were different. Those three Alters manifested themselves very often and interacted in Lina's therapy.

Eventually, I became more acquainted with two different characters: The Angry One and the No One. They were not two different personalities, as I first thought. The Angry One was created as a "split" of the No One. He was able to show powerful manifestations of outrage, without destruction as in the outbursts of the No One.

The No One and the Angry One were partially controlled by another powerful personality, the one known as The Guardian. I was told by the Wise One that if the Male Guardian lost control of the other two, mainly over the No One, or eventually became allied with them, their destructiveness would become chaotic toward any object or person in the room, up to and including homicide. Moreover, they could become out of control very easily if antagonized or provoked.

Little did I know then that this actually happened shortly before Lina entered into therapy with me.

At this point, I was indeed somewhat apprehensive. I was concerned about what was the best way to proceed, what type of approach or modality I should follow. I did not want to provoke more turmoil or cause more damage, especially since earilier that year a crisis occurred that lasted for two years involving one of my patients who wanted to kill several co-workers. After dealing with lawyers and the court system, I was not willing to be embroiled in another case with potential for so much destruction and violence.

So I negotiated new and drastic terms for Lina and the Personalities: no violence, no threats, no destructive behavior, and no harm to herself or others. I promised to avoid, as much as I could, any inpatient hospitalization for them, noting the horrible experiences they had suffered in the past. In spite of knowing that those Personalities were struggling for independence and individuality, logic told me that they were interconnected and connected with Lina—she had created them. So I talked to Lina, knowing that all of the Personalities were aware of what was going on. I told Lina to give me her answer at the next week's session.

At the same time, I encouraged the Alters, any one of "them," to come to the surface and voice their objections if they had any. I also promised to avoid psychotropic medications as much as possible. After all, what medications could I prescribe for whom? We were able to identify around eight basic personalities, with splitting to many others. What drugs could be used for the soft-spoken Wise One, or the threatening and vociferous No One and his creation "The Angry One," or the sweet six year old Lynny Sue, or the Bitch, or the She?

Even with the demand of no violence from "them" and the promise from me, which deep in my heart I meant to honor, I was still not sure that the therapy was going to work. Violence was an ever-present concern, and the future need for strong medications was entirely possible, although, if my promises were broken, maybe that would be my way out of my therapeutic involvement.

I did break my promise on February 9, 1993, because of Lina's severe suicidal ideations. She was hospitalized and discharged five days later, calmer and not suicidal. To my surprise, no Alter asked for my dismissal as therapist because of this broken promise.

I asked Lina why I was trusted, and she told me that it related to a session with Lynny Sue. She was describing the sexual abuse Lina had been exposed to as a child and the Alters noticed tears coming from my eyes. That won me the Alters' respect, since this was the first time anyone had ever cried for their pain. The Caretaker and the Wise One decided I was an exception to all the other doctors, counselors, and adults in Lina's life. This was the first time their feelings were not laughed at, a very important moment in their lives. I remembered feeling very sad, and at the same time angry, listening to Lynny Sue and seeing her suffer while describing some of the abuse.

Among the Alters was the She, who was very quiet, and pitiful. I have tried to remember her face. I have even reviewed the videotapes that I took while in therapeutic sessions with Lina, but I cannot precisely describe her physical appearance. After I learned about her existence, I tried many times to deal with her. I tried to bring her to the surface and have a one-on-one encounter with her, but I did not have any success. That made my job more difficult.

I was told by the "others" that she represented guilt, shame, pain, and the need for self-punishment and destruction — destruction of self and, consequently, destruction of the others. The She had frequent suicidal thoughts, with self-inflicted lacerations. Some of the Alters, I do not remember who, stated that, "Sometimes absence of pain, numbness of emotions is horrible, and self-mutilation is the only way to feel something."

When I heard that, I felt both sad and angry at the same time, although I was not supposed to. Psychiatrists are supposed to keep an emotional equilibrium and to be objective. Yet, I needed to understand; I needed to protect; I needed to reassure the integrity of the "Core." As a self-preservation maneuver, I asked the No One and the male Guardian to keep an eye on the She and to keep her at bay. It was obvious that the risk of suicide was high at that time.

As I said before, the Guardian and the No One were the two most powerful Personalities. The Guardian kept the No One in line, preventing more frequent manifestations of violence and destruction. However, the No One resented being subjugated by the Guardian. Somehow, I was able to get them, not necessarily integrated, but at least allied with a common goal — survival. If the She succeeded in convincing Lina to kill herself, all of them would be gone for good. They would die with her and this was something they didn't want to happen. Now they were fully aware of this.

CHAPTER TWO

TRIED TO BE LOVED

Lina's main complaint, among others, was "dissociation of memories and feelings." For instance, her mother gave her a picture of herself as a child, but Lina had no feelings and no memory of the event in the photo, no sequence, either before or after. At other times, she experienced a "goose flesh" feeling, with fear, tears, and apprehension, although she couldn't tell why she was having these distressing feelings without any recollection of memories or events.

But a six year old child would come to our aid.

I needed to know the age of each of the Alters, when they were created, and for what purpose. They should be able to recall memories hidden behind the Wall.

In order to learn about past events and collect data for therapeutic purposes, regressive hypnosis techniques can be used. Some therapists use the sodium amytal interview. The memory elicited by those methods usually provokes tremendous distress and turmoil, so the use of powerful sedatives is also necessary, and, at times, physical restraints are used to control the patient.

At the same time, this provokes resentment and adds more physical and emotional trauma to a patient already traumatized by past events. For these reasons, and because of my promise to avoid medications as much as possible, I decided not to use those methods.

Instead, as a trial, I asked Lina to start writing whatever came to her mind, and then we would begin working with those recollections. Lina's husband told me that she was very skillful with her hands. He could not understand this because she had chronic arthritis in her hands and fingers, but she was very creative at building miniature dollhouses and small furniture with great detail. She was also good at typing and working with the computer they had at home.

Based on that information, I encouraged her to start writing whatever came to her mind, or anything she could remember I wanted to know, I needed to know, of events that occurred when she was young. I was trying to find out how much she could remember about what had happened in the early years of her life.

She spoke in a soft, masculine tone, reflecting deep concern. "I see you need to know."

This took me by surprise. I interrupted and asked "him," "Who are you?"

"I'm the Wise One. I don't know what did happen. She was very young. I was not there, but I will try to get you someone who can help, someone who was there."

It was while we were negotiating the above, and while she was struggling to match fragmented old memories with real, distressing feelings, that I saw Lina change drastically in posture, voice, and attitude. She spoke in a soft, childish voice, with a childish expression on her face. She leaned forward and put her cheek on the desk and smiled.

I asked her, "Who are you? What is your name"?

She answered, "I'm Lynny Sue."

I was not shocked, but I was taken back at such a drastic change. How was Lina able to do that? Was she trying to fool me or was she joking? I think that my face showed my doubt. She continued exhibiting a smile that was the face of an innocent child, and when I asked her age, she told me she was six years old.

I offered Lynny Sue coloring crayons and paper and asked her to draw pictures. She tried to paint what appeared to be a house. She was very pleasant and conversational, saying, "Mommy loves me. I am a good girl. When I die I will go to Heaven."

I asked her if this drawing was of a house.

"Oh yeah," the little girl said.

I asked, "Is this a pig house?"

At this point, a severe emotional storm was unleashed. She started screaming and crying. Grabbing the crayon with her whole fist, she made strokes over the paper, trying to destroy the drawing of the house, and shouting over and over, "You don't go there, you don't go there, you are bad, you are going to burn in Hell! Mommy doesn't love you! My Mommy loves me, but Lina is going to Hell."

I tried to calm her down, so I asked her, "How old is Lina?"

The answer was, "She is four years old and Mommy hates her. Mommy loves me. She is going to Hell."

Now I was shocked and saddened watching the sudden changes within her. As she continued crying, I tried to hold her hands, but with a jerking movement she withdrew them and repeated several times, "No one loves me."

I told her, "You are a good girl. You are not bad; you are a child. Your Mommy loves you; I love you." Then I threw out a guess and told her, "The No Toe is the bad one. He is the one who needs to be punished and hated for his wrong doings."

Shortly after, Lynny Sue calmed down and disappeared almost as fast as she had appeared. I continued dealing with Lina.

Lynny Sue's Drawing

She was very quiet, with a very sad expression. She was starting to develop a partial awareness of those past events.

CHAPTER THREE

THE WISE ONE. THE NO ONE. LYNNY SUE.

I asked Lina to bring to therapy every week whatever she was writing at home. She brought some typed notes, nothing handwritten, but it was clear that, at times, the context changed and the writer would identify himself or herself.

What follows is a typed report by Lina.

> "It was November of 1992, and I was again in a deep depression. Maybe it was the holidays coming up; I didn't know what. That was not surprising. I seemed to always be depressed. I had accepted that I could not remember things. I tried to deal with those voices, the almost constant voices, always there. The shadows would flash through my mind. My husband is a recovering alcoholic, who also suffers from depression and he was seeing Dr. H. My husband suggested that I, too, start seeing him, but I was not willing to start again with yet another doctor. Long ago I had given up on them being able to help me, plus somewhere inside of me there was a great hatred of them. I had been with so many, and I spent many years in

> therapy, and it never seemed to help. I could feel somewhat good for a short time and all at once sink into a pit of depression."

(At this point something happened to the writing):

> "I must identify myself here. I am taking over. I'm the one who knows; I'm the Wise One. Lina has good reason to hate doctors. Didn't the 'ones in white' tell her if she did not stop crying they would give her a shot! Didn't she have the right to be frightened? That thing in that room was not her mother; that was a monster. Did any of those self-righteous people in white try to understand her screams? NO! All they wanted was to quiet her by threatening her more. This was not the first time her mother had left and returned different. At age five, it was difficult, very difficult to understand what had happened."

While I was reading and reviewing the above statements, Lina couldn't remember what the Wise One wrote.

I told her, "You see, you started writing and then the context changed. Don't you remember somebody else taking over?"

Then her voice changed drastically, becoming really deep, sarcastic, and grave, "I was the one who wrote that. I took over."

I asked, "Who are you?"

"I'm the No One," the voice said.

(The following pages show the shifting of the handwriting).

That voice matched Lina's very angry countenance. There was a complete change in her facial expression. The eyebrows became almost a straight line, while the eyes went deep into the sockets, shining with a powerful, penetrating look, deeply charged with hatred. The frame of the face became triangular. Her lips were tightly closed and her body reminded me of a boxer sitting in his corner and waiting for the bell to ring, ready to jump and attack a contender.

17

It is now Sunday but I wish to write about something th... happen yesterday We were going to drop —— off at his melting I helped him set up of course I have done it before but again I must be told exactly like it should be done. He had brought a tape for Steves birthday but he wouned not play it always "I ta you do it" He embosses me to no end if I say something I am being short wiit him and he starts "Pleas don't start in one me today Please just try a little bit to be my friend". Why must I always have to give in to him. Why must everything be his way Why can't I say anything I am always to afraid it will start a fight I hate to be yelled at I can't stand to be corrected all the time one everything from the way I walk to the way I say something. I experince a connection (for a lack of a better word) between past "feeling" and now. It was like that before ~~afraid~~ afraid to rock the boat, afraid I might do something to set off another fight. There were so many. I saw a young girl, she had long brown hair, brown eyes so full of saddness

how can I reach her to bring her comfort. I
don't believe it was wise to tell her of this
yet. Things are not well within. We need
her stronger not weaker. She fears so much
she is so fragile at this time. Things are
not going well. She wishes closeness but
fears that which she never had. She wishes
to talk to express her feelings but she does not
know how. She fights herself. She fears rejection
to the point of being always afraid. She
needs to be accepted yet fears if you really
knew her you would dislike her. Always on
guard, always afraid. I fear the point when
she cares not for anything. Have you not notice
she is withdrawing more and more. She spends
more and more time within. I grieve so
for her she suffers so. You cannot help her
What do you think you can accomplish
with this nonsense How foolish
you all are. What do you think
you can accomplish! You listen
to his words Have you not learned
how easily words are said!
You who still wishes to believe
in good in all people That
fairy tales all come true that

Everyone has a happy ending!!
Those words were altered not
all fairy tales had happy even
often endings. You listen to
~~that~~ one who doesn't under
stand us Who did not even
believe until us and yet you
trust you believe his words.
Has not the past taught you
anything Did not ~~the~~ others
listen Did not the others
pretend to care Did not ~~the~~
others have pretty words
What happened then —
Betrayal - hurt - pain and
yet you trust again! I know
you he is yet just a Human
Being after all. We protect
and he does not — Did
she not prove ~~that~~ today
Have we not had to take
away the pain again! She
is not ready We are not yet
ready ~~Leave things~~ as they
all for none. He has not
even scratched the surface

have we made a mistake. Its a hell of time to ask that! You would not listen to me. You would not heed my warnings. He likes me big fucking deal you medlers you idiots! You you you who tells me to sit back he have let you handle things look at the mess you have created! You fucking Kept us all. She was safe! She was protected from all that would harm But you all ~~thought~~ different Now She has no safe place Now she has no haven to go to you listen to words again How dare you. You have put your trust in another again He is not of us He has ~~not~~ the ~~wonder~~ stonely He has not the Knowledge How can you trust a smiling face spouting words He behind I am his friend things will get beyond ~~our~~ our control and ~~then~~ what! You give him to much power. You trust him to much!!

Will we never be able to convince him or can we always control him. I hope so. We can not forever keep him at bay. I do hope we have done the right thing. We must trust we must not ever lose aim. We must keep our hope alive.

WISE ONE AGAIN

...

Why Won't they Leave us Alone

Can't Take this much More

Must do something about this anger building up! So much were is their peace where is an ending

to all this maddness they call life!!
So much pain never ending anymore.
need it all to go away. I ~~fee~~
feel so angry so tore (a battle
wages. hand shakes so bad I can
hardly write. When will it get
better? I am begining to believe that
it isn't. Things will always be
the way they are. The peace we need will
never come. So many mistakes, so many
changes have we made and none has
worked. Things are really bad. Whats to be
done.

I tried to establish direct verbal communication with this powerful personality, who for the first time had come to the surface and spoken directly to me. I was very cautious in my questions, thinking twice about each one, and being careful with the words I was using. It was disturbing to see someone with so much anger and hatred, who could be potentially homicidal. I was anxious not to provoke him. At the same time, however, I wanted and needed his cooperation.

I approached him, "I'm dealing with and treating Lina, who is a woman. Why are you within her representing a powerful masculine figure? And this question I'm asking you also applies to the other masculine Personalities or Alters, the Wise One, the Male Guardian, the Angry One."

The same voice answered, "We are old-fashioned. Masculinity is a symbol of strength, and weakness is characteristic of females. We need to be strong. We need to be powerful."

After that short intervention, the No One disappeared.

Therapy continued. Lina was coming once a week for one and a half hours of therapy, and sometimes the sessions lasted closer to two hours. She was always the last appointment because I considered the outcome of every session to be unpredictable. That was the only time of the day my secretary was instructed not to interrupt. Lina was very fragile. Alters or Personalities were coming and going, and minimal distraction was enough to make them disappear.

It is important to mention other problems that Lina was going through besides her MPD and dealing with a foggy, traumatic, distressing past history. She showed an extreme need to deal with current problems. She had difficulties accepting her mother's demanding attitude, which constantly provoked guilty feelings. Lina also felt manipulated by her sisters and her own children. On the other hand, the more the therapy was progressing with Lina showing more control and not "escaping," or experiencing "time lost," her husband was showing more signs of insecurity, to the extent of complaining to me (and to her) that "she was going to leave him at any time." He said this regardless of the fact that she had not disappeared for any length of time while in therapy.

Though in many sessions, the therapy was geared to help Lina deal with actual problems such as dilemmas she was having or interacting with her family, it became increasingly evident that those problems were closely connected to her past, since even while dealing with current problems, the Alters would come to the surface and interact with me. Lina was more and more aware of this intervention, and as it happened, this mix of treating past and present problems enhanced the healing process.

A few months after therapy started, I became engaged in a sort of unilateral shouting match with one Alter who identified himself as the Angry One. He was cursing and blaming society for what happened to Lina, denying the existence of "what people call God." He would ask, "What type of God is this who allows so many ugly things to happen? If He is as powerful as many people think He is, why doesn't He stop it? Either He doesn't care or He doesn't exist."

As the Angry One talked, he would lean against the edge of the desk and pound the palm of his hand against the top of the desk. His voice was loud and breathless, and gave me no opportunity to reply. Regardless of what appeared to be his hostile attitude, I did not feel threatened, and I tried to steer his theological topic to more tangible ground. I asked the Angry One his age and asked him also to be more specific in his statements, at which time he became more annoyed. In a deep tone of voice he asked me, "Why do you want to know? We will not permit any more pain or suffering."

I told him, "I'm trying to mitigate Lina's pain. I'm trying to make her understand and help her face some unresolved matters in her life. But if I don't know, and if she doesn't know, then what?"

After a few seconds of silence he added, "So, you want to know."

"Yes," I said, "I need to, if you want me to help you all."

Suddenly, a couple of drastic changes occurred. First the hostility disappeared from Lina's face and her attitude became more peaceful and serene. Then almost immediately, she took on the voice and gestures of a female child. I asked this Alter for a name and why she decided to take over.

"I'm Lynny Sue— remember me?"

"Yes I do. Why are you here?" I asked.

The answer caught me off guard.

"The Female Guardian sent me to talk with you. I was there; I know what happened."

The Female Guardian was mentioned to me in the past more than once, but this was the very first time she was reported as taking part in the treatment.

"Lizzy liked to play games with No Toe. She is going to burn in Hell."

I asked her, "Who is Lizzy?"

"She is four years old."

I did not mention "the Pig House," avoiding the possibility of unleashing another crisis, but I asked Lynny Sue about No Toe. She told me that he used to go barefoot, and his big toe was missing. Then she added, "He used to hang around a swimming pool with another big, fat man."

I was talking with a six or seven year old girl, who was trying to shift blame onto a four year old child. My approach was to let her consider that she was Lina at age six, but also the same Lina at age four. She was extremely reluctant to accept any relationship between herself and the four year old. It sounded like an older sister describing a younger sister's sinful, horrible behavior. I avoided asking more questions even though I had spent time trying to convince her that Lynny Sue and Lizzy were both Lina at different ages.

What follows is a copy of my progress note from that session of psychotherapy:

> This afternoon my session with Lina lasted for over two hours. Trying to integrate Lynny Sue (six years old) with the four year old child, making them both one entity, and at the same time trying to mitigate the feelings of guilt and blame, shifting the responsibility away from the children and placing the blame of the wrong doing where it belonged — On No Toe and another fellow who used to hang around a swimming pool and take advantage of young girls.
>
> It was evident that among the Alters, levels of control or hierarchy existed and were accepted, but not without some resentment. What follows will again show the validity of this statement.

Another shifting took place and from Lynny Sue another Personality or Alter came to the surface. It was the face of a female showing pain, hopelessness, despair and frustration. She started talking, softly and slowly. Although I did not remember seeing her before, I could identify her as the She, representing guilt, the "need" for punishment, and self-destruction as the only way to end the suffering and the tormented memories.

I restrained myself and did not call her by the name the other Alters had given her [The She]. I wanted to get in a direct confrontation with her. I wanted to tell her how stupid her performance was, but I was afraid she would become frightened and disappear in the darkness of Lina's mind. I did not talk. I listened to her and the more I listened, the more I felt sorry for her suffering and anguish.

I remember looking straight into her eyes while moving my hands as if asking a question, but before I uttered any word she said, "Pain in the mind is worse, much worse than pain in the body. When I see blood, then I know that there is some pain in the body. I will try to stop this misery. It has to end. We cannot endure it anymore."

It was Lina talking with a tone of voice that I had not heard before. Indeed, this was suicidal talk. It was a cry for help from someone at the end of their rope. It was very sad. She was feeling hopeless and helpless, and what was more distressing was that this frame of mind and her statements felt like they were spilling and spreading all around her.

At any other time or during any other type of psychiatric engagement, that attitude was enough to merit consideration for hospitalization in a psychiatric setting to protect her from attempting to harm herself. I did not do it this time. Why? I don't know. It was risky, but maybe I trusted myself, or maybe I trusted that the other Guardians and the other Personalities could keep the She at bay.

This session of psychotherapy was indeed very challenging and left me, at that time, without specific answers. I went home feeling sad. That was bad. We are trained to "be detached." Beware of developing sympathy. Transference? Yes! Empathy? Careful! Watch your own emotions!

I was amazed. So many months working with Lina, and still I was not used to those changes, but I was able to see the differences among them. Then I asked myself, and later on I asked her, if her husband was able to detect the changes.

The Wise One was the one who answered me, "Her husband thinks that sometimes she acts in a very nasty manner, not knowing that he was most probably interacting with the No One, or maybe the Angry One. When the Bitch was in charge, he complained that she was insolent and antagonistic. Other times, she showed childish manners and behavior. This was Lynny Sue, who, by the way, is very skillful at making miniature dollhouses." The Wise One continued saying, "Sometimes she acts like a crazy person, cutting herself in order to bleed and wanting to die, and she has tried that several times. The She is the one who is doing this."

The next week, Lina's husband came to see me for follow-up on his own treatment. I asked him the same question and he gave me similar answers. He was indeed having problems understanding that he was married to one person who had different personalities, and he was not convinced of Lina's MPD problem. He was fighting his own feelings and felt neglected. He was losing control of Lina, and could not understand that sex was not a driving force for her, and never was. How could it be when sex was in great part to blame for her messy and miserable life?

It seemed as if tenderness and compassion were absent from him. He felt he was nice, and that she was not receptive. The truth is he tried many times to have sex with her by force and Lina's reaction was the surfacing of the No One, so intensely that at one time, she had tried to kill him. When violence was not present, the Bitch answered his complaints.

Lina's husband Allen was generally a nice guy. He was going daily to Alcoholics Anonymous (A.A.) meetings, and was dry. He was not drinking, but he was not sober. He was what people in A.A. call a "dry drunk." Sobriety is dealing with the frequent stressors of life and accepting it. Allen was haunted with insecurity at home and at work, carrying scars from his service in Viet Nam. He presented himself with a sort of "acceptance" attitude, but it was masking deep, emotional conflict. He was afraid his wife Lina would walk away from him once she felt secure and took control of her life.

Once the person stops drinking, he is never said to be a recovered alcoholic. He is a "recovering" alcoholic, because alcohol dependency is a disease, and its only effective treatment is not to drink. This process goes on for the entire remaining life of the alcoholic. The only effective treatment to prevent relapse is to avoid the first drink once the individual has entered into the recovery process.

I have seen patients who were recovering for 20 years, and then take a drink. Only one drink of alcohol is enough to relapse in a short time and become a worse alcoholic than before.

I was extremely concerned about Allen having that first drink. He was sure that he would rather be "dead than drunk again."

CHAPTER FOUR

THE WOMAN

It was a hot summer day. The cooling system unit in my office was turned off because it made too much noise. Most of the time, Lina was on time for her appointments, but that day she was a few minutes late. I was writing some notes regarding the patient I had seen before her.

She knocked at the door and entered without being invited in. This was quite different from other times when she used to enter quietly, even shyly, avoiding eye contact. Most of the time she would dress nicely, but with no makeup. Many times she looked as if she did not have the time to dress fashionably.

This afternoon, as she entered the room, her gait was different, with sinuous, winding movements of her body. Every step was rather slow, and I may say, well calculated. She sat in her usual chair with elegance, looked straight into my eyes and smiled, in a provocative manner.

I told her, "You look different today."

Her answer was, "Yes, I am," and she put the emphasis on the "I am" while placing on my desk a folder containing several papers written in different styles. There were four different handwritings, and she was able to identify one of them as written by the No One.

I asked this new Alter for her name and why she had come. She called herself the Woman and said she had come to meet me.

"Why the name of Woman," I asked her?

"I'm the one who likes sex, and that is why I am not welcomed by "the others."

I told her there is nothing wrong with sex, and she said, "That is what you think, but they can not handle it."

At the same time she was rubbing her hand against the skin of her shoulder and lower neck. I asked her, "What are you doing?"

"It is hot in here," she said. At the same time, she was crossing her legs in a manner I considered provocative.

It was clear that this Personality was trying to be sexy and seductive. I did not remember Lina acting like that before, but nevertheless, at this moment I called her Lina.

She objected, "I'm the Woman; I am not her."

I insisted on calling her Lina Woman or Woman Lina, and after a while, she agreed. She did not like Lina, my patient, because of the way that she acted, her shabby appearance, her need to please, easygoing manner, and hidden emotions.

I asked her, "Why did you come this time? What happened?"

"The other Alters were too busy discussing and protecting Lina because of the turmoil she is going through, so I took the opportunity to come to the surface to meet and talk with you."

I asked myself if this Alter — the Woman — was a continuum of Rowdy, the teenager, but without the wild lifestyle of Rowdy. She should know enough about Lina's past life, so she could give me data regarding what happened to Lina in her early years. I needed to know more about her family background, especially her relationship with her father. I wanted to know more about her mother, her sisters, and her childhood. The

Woman did indeed help me. She was eager to talk, giving me a lot of information.

Her father was described as an alcohol abuser and perhaps chronically intoxicated. He was loud, violent and, at times, threatened the family with a shotgun. He apparently did not abuse her sexually. The Woman described her mother as possibly promiscuous, bringing home men when her husband was not at home. She introduced them as Lina's "uncles." Though I still didn't have a clear picture of the situation, it was a possibility that some of those "uncles" might have taken advantage of Lina.

Also I learned more about No Toe. He was not a Personality or a byproduct of a tormented mind. He did exist. He was real and had abused her many times. He forced her to perform sexual acts that traumatized her for the rest of her life and this was one of the biggest factors in unleashing the horrible nightmare, confusion, and turmoil that Lina had been going through for so many years.

The Woman cooperated without too much hesitation. She described with more detail, what, to some extent, Lynny Sue had mentioned before.

Most of the incidents happened in a place named the "Pig House," a place like a barn or something similar. The man who was there was barefoot, and Lina was able to remember, through the Alters or perhaps flashbacks, that this man had a missing toe on his foot. There was also another older man who was described as hanging around a swimming pool and taking advantage of youngsters and teenage girls. He also was "playing games" with Lina, games that she was too ashamed to recall. She was constantly blaming herself, putting all of the guilt and blame on a four year old girl.

Due to my need to be out of town two days after this session, I asked the Woman how much she thought Lina could be made aware of the information she had given me. Her comment was, "I don't care."

This Alter was very reluctant to be identified with her creator, and it took the better part of the session to try to integrate this aspect of the personality disorder. I think I was somewhat successful by the end or at least she was no longer showing signs of being annoyed or distressed. From time to time, she shrugged her shoulders, which I took as acceptance.

That afternoon I learned a lot about the Alters. The Woman mentioned the No One, saying that he was "playing a game" with me. The word "game" was repeated many times, and although the context was different, I felt uneasy. So I asked her, "What do you mean by that?"

She said, "He [The No One] is the master of playing games. He named himself No One because he doesn't need to respond to any questions asked. He doesn't need to answer for any of his outburst. He knows, but he pretends he doesn't know."

She couldn't tell me more about the type of game he was playing, or trying to play with me, or what he intended to accomplish by it. I told the Woman that her comments were making me feel uneasy and unhappy, because this was not a game. This was a very serious matter, and we were dealing with life and death.

The Woman said, "The No One is trying to control the whole situation because he is fearful of being wiped out. The Angry One was created by the Male Guardian to control possible outbursts of destructiveness from the No One. The Male Guardian is the most powerful, and he seems to be in control of the whole situation; he is in agreement that to avoid violence and destructiveness, he should cooperate with therapy and the therapist."

At this point, Lina's voice changed again. Now it was the voice of a male, with a deep sound, but with no threatening undertones. Lina had lost her feminine demeanor, and the entire sexual and seductive attitude disappeared — it was simply and suddenly gone.

Now a male was talking and gesturing, and without me asking him, he volunteered information. "I'm the one they call the Wise One," he said as he nodded in affirmative movements. The tone of his voice was calm and reassuring.

I learned to listen to him carefully. He conveyed the idea that the Angry One was not needed anymore and had no further arguments with which to justify his existence. There was no more need to show anger unless there was frustration or immediate threat. The Wise One did not mention the name of the No One. Was the Wise One fearful of provoking him?

I reassured them all that there was no threat coming from these sessions. When our time was ended, we negotiated my absence for the next week. It would be the first time that our weekly sessions were interrupted.

In this last paragraph I said that I was talking to "them," because at this point, I was convinced that in talking with one Alter, the others were listening, and at the same time, Lina would understand as well and be able to recall whatever I talked about with any Alter.

I gave Lina and her husband the name of the doctor who was covering for me while I was on vacation. I have to say that I left with hesitation and some level of anxiety. I did not want "them" to feel like I was abandoning them. I was not feeling comfortable going away because Lina was still very fragile, but I needed to take a break.

CHAPTER FIVE

I'M LOOKING AT YOU AND IT IS LIKE TWO PERSONS IN ME.

The "Wall" that for years was erected and sealed to block memories and protect Lina from the painful emotional and physical trauma of earlier years was already filtering through some clues here and there. At the same time, those memories were accompanied by anguishing feelings of insecurity, sadness, discomfort, and anger, but, so far, without outward or inward destructiveness, in spite of the No One's intervention and his hatred for Lina's family.

It seems that the Male Guardian was in charge. He indeed was my silent co-therapist while I was gone.

My vacation lasted for ten days. I made a couple of long distance calls to my office while I was out. Everything was okay, but I still felt uneasy leaving Lina, her family, her husband, and the Alters by themselves.

When I returned from vacation, Lina came to therapy that afternoon and asked me in a polite manner if I had had a good time. "It was good and relaxing, but I was worried about you and your husband," I answered.

"We are okay," she said, "but my father is very sick. He's in the hospital, and I feel very confused. The voices are back again. They were never completely gone, but now they are strong, and I can identify most of them."

Lina was starting to develop some awareness and was able to identify some of the voices of the different Alters and fragmented ones. She mentioned a new entity, the Gatekeeper, but without a definite profile of him.

I asked her, "Perhaps it is a combination of the Male and Female Guardians?"

That question was never answered, but I continued asking questions. If therapy was to continue, I need more information. Lina tried to cooperate, but she was either blocking on her own, or most probably, "someone" was interfering.

It is true that at the beginning of her treatment, she was hesitant regarding my approach. I used to feel that I was walking on eggshells, but after many months of therapy, I was feeling freer to ask and press for answers.

She mentioned having a "funny feeling," and while she was saying this, she had sort of an empty expression in her eyes. Then she added, "I'm looking at you, and it is like 'two persons' are in me."

"Who are those two persons?" I asked her. "Are they new? How long they have been there?"

She mentioned two more names as she tried to explain. One was "The Feeler," who could be sent to the surface by any Alter from the deeper side to explore. Then she added another name to the list, "The Doubter."

No definite profile was seen in these two new "visitors." I use the word visitors, because I didn't know if we were dealing with new Alters and I had no verbal communication with them. I did not see any drastic change in Lina's behavior, only a very short lived, "different" expression in her eyes.

Lina tried her best to explain, but just at that moment she started mumbling, "You are talking too much." Then she started speaking with a different tone of voice, and her attitude changed drastically again. Someone started talking about her father, "our father," who had a heart attack, alcoholism, and an aneurysm. Then she started giggling and laughing and I asked her what was so funny about that.

In a deep, rough tone of voice, pronouncing every word with hatred and bitterness, her answer was, "That son of a bitch is suffering, and we are glad. He was very abusive and we are glad to see him suffering and dying."

I didn't know who was talking. He could be either the No One or he could be the Angry One. To whoever was speaking, I said, "Lina's father is a very sick man. We don't know what really happened to him. It is true that he was very abusive, emotionally and physically, though not sexually. On the other hand, I do not have information that he was physically abusive or violent against Lina." There was no response to this statement.

Not everything among the Alters was negative and threatening. The Female Guardian did not talk directly to me, but she sent Lynny Sue and Lizzy as well as the Wise One whenever I was putting pressure on Lina to learn about the events of her younger years.

One day something very strange, even unique, happened while I was interacting with the children. I do not remember which of the children was speaking to me at the time. I remember that I started writing some brief notes, and when I looked again at Lina to continue talking with whichever child was speaking to me, she was sitting very relaxed, and her hair was shining with a rich golden tone. It was like the sunlight was filtering from behind her. It was afternoon, but the sun was not visible from the window of my office. I remember seeing Lina's face change Her face showed a very peaceful smile, reflecting tranquility. This was a new sight for me. It lasted only briefly, maybe a few seconds, and before I finished asking, "Who are you?" she had disappeared. That show of serenity was very pleasant. As I said, it lasted briefly, and then one of the children took over. I tried to interact with that "peaceful-faced personality" several times that day, but without any success. I asked one of the alters — I don't recall who — to identify this new entity. She was called the Protector of the Children. I was led to believe that she was afraid of being hurt again, as she had been many times in the past. I felt that this female was possibly a split of the Female Guardian and not a well-defined Alter.

After that session of therapy, looking at the beautiful change I saw in Lina's face reassured me that all of the time we had invested in therapy was worthwhile and had not been wasted.

The next week our session was again productive. It seemed that someone else had come to the surface and was identified by Lina later on as the Caretaker. Lina told me, "I'm looking at you, and it is as if 'another' within me is also looking at you. It is hard for me now to have a clear view of what is reality and what is not. My memory is foggy."

I wondered if the Caretaker was related to the Guardians. Was the name Gate Keeper common for both the Female and Male Guardian? Did it also apply to the Protectors? A few weeks earlier, when she had the same experience while looking at me, she had given me names of the Feeler and the Doubter, as those who came "to explore." Now, with the same type of look in her eyes, the name given was Gate Keeper.

I did not ask more questions. I let her talk. I was careful not to make any remark or "contribution" which could be taken as my full acceptance of placing those new entities at the same level of the other Alters, who were already well-established and well-defined.

Then she started mentioning more names. "Ted, he is an alcoholic. Benny is violent." These were two of her four sons from a previous marriage.

Her voice changed again, and the Wise One took over. "She has a fear of intimacy. The No Toe abused her, and also another older man." [The name of Lina's neighbor was mentioned here.]

Again, her voice shifted to an angry, hostile pitch, and I was not sure if it was the No One. "Her mother will pay, same token. Isolation."

I asked, "What happened, why that anger, why the refusal to communicate?"

I told "them" at this session, "If you guys do not remember, there is no justification at all to be raising hell for what you 'think' happened, so, stop playing games."

In subsequent weeks, Lina was allowed by the Alters to remember most of their conversations with me every time they came to the surface. They were accepting little by little her participation in "their" therapy and her ability to remember most of my conversation with them. In this way, Lina was becoming more aware and developing insight into past events of her life and facing her reactions and feelings. She was developing tools to solve actual problems and stressful situations without the need to escape and allow an Alter to take over. I felt good. Therapy seemed to be rendering positive results. No turmoil was reported. No splitting headaches. No time lost.

I continued providing therapy to Allen, Lina's husband. He still felt uneasy regarding Lina's behavior. "She is not showing those flares of outrage that she use to have so frequently in the past. Now she finds answers for everything I say."

He also told me that Lina was different. I asked him to be more specific.

"Not only the way she talks, like 'bitching' sometimes, but also the way she dresses now and all the time she takes before she goes out."

More than once, at home, he complained that his wife showed a sort of antagonistic attitude which he called "bitching."

Maybe she was learning to be more assertive, and that was new for him.

I asked him, "Could it be that she is now more assertive?"

His answer was, "She is different."

"Of course she is," I told him.

Later I learned that when they were first married, he tried to control her in many ways that were unacceptable to her, but she never voiced her discontent. At the present time, he felt himself loosing ground in that area. He didn't realize that he was living with a more stable wife. His controlling behavior had provoked anger and hatred within the Alters in the past, so much anger and hatred that the No One thought of him with murderous intent.

That afternoon I told Allen, "When you first asked me to work with your wife, I was very reluctant to do it, but you insisted. Today I think you feel I am not giving you the same amount of time or care I'm giving her. It is true; I am not. She is a very difficult case for me. When I see you in therapy, I can go home and relax. When I see her, many times I go home very tired, worried, and trying to predict and think ahead of time what will be next?"

I continued, "I have seen changes in Lina, positive changes. She is different. She is much better. You may not like the way she is now, but you will have to start learning how to deal with a 'new' wife."

I promised him that I would talk with Lina at her next appointment to find out what she thought was happening in her marriage.

When she came to our session the following week, she was elegant and feminine like the Woman, but without the sexual innuendos and seductiveness. To my surprise, she extended her arm and gave me a firm handshake when she entered the room. Shaking hands with Lina almost never occurred during the first few month of therapy, and when it did happen, it was always initiated by me.

I smiled and I asked, "Who is the visitor today?"

She said, "I'm the Lady. I'm very close to Lina. I'm trying to teach her how to dress, how to shop, how to combine colors properly." She added, "She is so careless and, at times, sloppy."

I was tempted to ask this new Personality, what type of relationship existed between her and the Woman, but I decided not to. The answer could be like opening a Pandora's Box. They both took me by surprise. They were coming and going without too much interaction with me, since I was not used to them.

While I was talking with the Lady, I asked her a question that was aimed at Lina.

I asked her how her husband was handling the changes.

"Not too good," she said. "Seems that he thinks I will leave him. *I* don't know why he feels that way. He is a good man. *I* love him. He likes me quiet. He doesn't like me talking back to him."

By saying "I," The Lady bonded with Lina, which was interpreted by me as and integration. Now I needed to know what was going to happen to the Woman and to the Bitch. Would they try to develop independent personalities or would they stay "split." Those Personalities grew with the Core, and I couldn't tell which one of them was deep-rooted or predominant. How were they going to integrate and combine into one?

I remembered the promise I made to Lina's husband regarding the "strong" attitude that Lina was showing more often and, of course, I was avoiding any questions leading to turmoil or distress.

"No," I thought to myself, "I will not ask her today." The session was going really well, and I was not willing to bring out any clouds. Nevertheless, I did ask the Lady if she was connected to the Angry One.

"You know that we all are, but I'm not him. Why are you asking?"

The tone of her voice changed noticeably when she asked that question, though I did not observe any drastic change in Lina's face or body posture. It sounded simply like she was defensive or annoyed.

I told her, "I was talking with Allen last week, and he told me about your attitude sometimes."

"Oh yeah! I bitch! That is what I do. That is what I am. They call me the Bitch. I can speak for myself, but I am not the Angry One. No need to be like him."

"Oh, I see," was my only comment.

And after that, the Bitch was gone. Even today, I do not know who the principal personality was — maybe it was the Lady or perhaps the Woman and the Bitch were the splits. I knew that deep in Lina's heart she wanted to be a little bit of all of them.

From there on, it was really difficult most of the time to tell the difference between Lina and the Lady. Purposely, while I was addressing the Lady, I was calling her Lina. I don't know if that was a quick fix or not, but from that week on, she came to the office dressed in a more attractive manner.

That afternoon I was again feeling really good and more confident regarding the outcome of the therapy. At home that night, my wife who was working with me in the office, told me that she noticed the change in Lina and reported her to be more talkative and friendly in the waiting room.

I need to mention that many "names" came to the surface. At times it was confusing, but it seemed that we managed to be selective and were able to give enough time and attention to those Alters important enough to influence the outcome of the therapy and also to those who were willing or able to give importnat data or information. It was challenging and stressful, but in the end, it showed good results.

CHAPTER SIX

THE SEARCH FOR LINA

Lina continued typing her own history and documenting how her treatment with me began. She seemed to be in better control of herself, but her typing, at times, was done by the Wise One because Lina did not have recollection or clear memories of the early years of her life as she tried to explain the origins of the Protectors. Those memories of early traumatic experiences and abuse were contained by the Wall. There were Guardians watching that Wall and preventing memories from coming to the surface.

(These are Lina's words):

> Where to begin? It seems to me that I have been asking that question all of my forty two years of life. What is the one thing that makes a person an individual? I have a condition defined as Multiple Personality Disorder. I had very few memories that were mine, and yet they were all there being kept for me. I guess the normal thing to do would be to start at the beginning. For me, this was the hardest part, for I could not remember any beginning, I just was. After two years of therapy, I'm just learning what the beginning was. The search for Lina Y. has been going

on for the last twenty two years. [Note: The initial Y. is used in order to protect her identity.]

As hard as it was for me to accept or believe that I am a MPD, I do believe it was harder for Dr. H. Until I became his patient, he was a nonbeliever. Thanks to him, I am at last finding freedom. Freedom from so many unknown fears, the freedom to be me, the freedom to do more than merely survive, I'm finally able to look at the past, deal with it and let it go.

I started writing as part of my therapy. I have not written this alone, for I have never been alone, I have had "Protectors" almost from birth it seems. With the help of Dr. H., I have finally met them all—so different and yet all alike in their struggle to not only protect Lina Y., but to survive. I haven't always known that I was different, that everyone wasn't like me. I really don't know exactly when I realized that truth. All I actually knew was that somehow I was forty two years old, but could only remember the last seven years, and it was only a partial recall!

Well let's begin!

It was November of 1992. I tried to explain my frame of mind and feelings, but someone took over without my active participation or conscious request. The Wise One took over. He tried to explain the fear of doctors and hospitals, and all the turmoil surrounding my mother's sickness. Another powerful Alter showed his presence. The No One was remarkable. He did not want more therapy. In his fear of disappearing, he was threatening, and today I strongly feel that this is why the co-therapist that Dr. H. hired quit on me. The No One chased him out.

My memory is foggy, but I am trying to remember the first time I met Dr. H. It was very brief, in the hospital, where my husband was receiving treatment for alcoholism and Dr. H. was his attending physician. It was like family therapy, but in this case, the family was Allen and I. I do not remember what was discussed or suggested in that first meeting. "

The second time I met him when I went with my husband to one of his sessions as an outpatient at Dr. H.'s office. He had Allen on some medication for his mood swings. He really seemed to be helping him. Allen liked him and trusted him. I cannot really explain why I trusted Dr. H. at first. It is so confusing. I went with Allen to see him because Allen almost pushed me to go with him. I kept asking myself, "Do I really want to go through all of this again just to be given some pills?" I had little faith that there was any hope for me.

My husband knew something was wrong with me. He called it "mood swings." In a minute, I could transform myself into another person, changing my facial expression and attitude. Those drastic changes were so fast, that it was driving him crazy. "Lina," he was constantly telling me, "you really need help. You cannot continue like this." I tried to justify myself, but how could I do that if I did not know what was going on. I felt like a war was going inside of my head.

Then from somewhere deep inside there was a voice, "Yes, you must try. We cannot forever stay as we are." Finally, I gave in and went to see Dr. H. The first session was in December of 1992.

I do not remember much of the first visit with him. At that time, the "Shell" was in control and functioning for the Alters. [Shell seems to be a name given by Lina to describe a shield to protect herself from external emotional injury rather than referring to an Alter or Personality.]

I know that Dr. H. wrote down notes about the history I gave him and after we talked for about an hour, he admitted he wasn't quite sure where I fit. He set me up for some tests and gave me a prescription to help slow down my thoughts. "Right again, just a quick fix." That's what I thought at that time. He also sent me to see one of the co-therapists in his office and requested records from previous hospitalizations and therapy. Looking back, I am so glad that both Dr. H. and the Wise One didn't just give up. Dr. H. was the first "shrink" that looked past the obvious. He questioned himself and asked for help to help me. There had never been anyone before who had said, "I'm just not sure. Let's do some testing."

I saw Dr. H.'s co-therapist a couple of times. I remember sitting in her office and she asked me if I remembered putting my head down on her desk, and I admitted I did not. Now I know it was Lynny Sue who came that day.

The co-therapist told me about a lady she knew whose hand did not have any feeling. At that point, something clicked. I told her my whole body was like that. I could cut myself and not even realize it until I saw the blood. Even my family doctor had remarked about my high tolerance for pain. (Yet the headaches were terrible.)

This lady co-therapist knew me, and for some reason it terrified me. She asked me if I had heard of Multiple Personality Disorder. Of course, who had not heard about Sybil? I had even read the book years ago. It had not impressed me.

Dr. H. had received a copy of my records. It showed my past history of suicide attempts. I did not remember being hospitalized so many times. As I said before,

I had only partial awareness of the last seven years of my life."

That day in his office, I had visions of a room full of children — seven little girls. A rocking chair was in the center of the room. There was a window. Looking out, you could see a beautiful field of wild grass and wildflowers. I was immersed in sorrow. I felt like crying, but I don't cry (at least then I could not cry). There was a young lady who came to me. She was the Caregiver. I was not sure then what that vision meant.

When results of the tests were available, I met again with Dr. H., my husband and the co-therapist. I was diagnosed as suffering from classic MPD. The co-therapist did not feel really qualified to deal with me, and Dr. H. had never worked with any patient with that type of problem.

Dr. H. brought in a psychiatric R.N., with a Master's degree in Counseling, who was working with him at some other place. According to Dr. H., this person had broad experiences working with patients suffering from Post Traumatic Stress Disorders as a consequence of abuse in early childhood and satanic cult involvement in early life. I was told that severe emotional suffering in the early years of my life resulted in the outcome of my psychological problems.

And the journey began.

When Lina brought the previous notes to discuss, she could not elaborate or explain who the Caregiver was that she mentioned. The Female Guardian, the Protector, and the Caregiver seem to have been created to protect the "children," or, I presume, to prevent the painful memories of childhood from being remembered in adulthood, triggering more guilty feelings, remorse and the need for self-punishment leading to self-destruction.

CHAPTER SEVEN

FAMILY HISTORY

What follows is the past history of Lina's life told mainly by the Wise One, through Lina's typing and through Lina's own memories. My comments also are included.

At this point, the Wise One is writing:

> Enough of that. Back where I left off. Ah, yes, "the beginning." How to explain so that Lina can understand. To understand, one must remember that we are dealing with children, even though some have been here for around forty years with a child's understanding and a child's emotions, not an adult's. Also, we are dealing with perceptions of that which are going around them.
>
> Things that would not be traumatic for one person could destroy another.

(Dr. H.): It seems to me that my therapy was rendering positive results. I did not try to minimize the trauma(s) that Lina went through, but I have mentioned very often her sensitivity and, consequently, her increased response to the emotional/physical distress she endured. With this approach, I tried not to take the blame away from the perpetrators, but to enable her to mitigate somehow the anger and hatred that she [and the Alters] had been harboring for so many years.

> (Wise One): How could a two year old child understand sickness? All Lina knew was that her mother went away. She could not understand that her mother was sick. Lina felt like she was abandoned, that her mother went away. When her mother returned, Lina could not understand why all of a sudden she was no longer loved, held, talked to, no more time for her.
>
> Grandfather took care of her, held her, and loved her while her mother was away. Mother came back home and she was pushed aside. No more time for Lina, Mother was taking care of the new baby [Lina's younger sister]. The new baby was the center of attention, no more room for Lina. How could she, at that age, grasp that her mother and the baby almost died. Her father was in Korea. All she knew was that he was not there. Also, she could not understand why she was no longer the "Apple" of her grandfather's eye. Lina was called a spoiled brat. She was "bad." So much pain and confusion. Why? What had she done that was so bad and wrong? She was not bad, but in her childish mind, she recognized that if you are sick or hurt, then people will care about you... here the seed for the "She" was planted.

(Dr. H.): The She is full of guilt and distress, and represents self-punishment, suicidal tendencies, and self-inflicted wounds that Lina was aware of only when blood was spilled.

> (Wise One): It was at this time that the idea of us (Alters) was forming. Lina was about three years old. She had no more loving grandparent to take care of her, someone who would always love her, care for her, protect her and never leave her! At this point in Lina's life, we were just a daydream.

(Dr. H.): In the following, Lina is the one writing, although I need to clarify once more that sometimes it is not Lina herself. The Alters controlled her thoughts, mood, speech, and behavior without Lina's volition.

> My father was a career military man. He spent twenty-one years in the service, which meant we spent twenty-one years in a military regime. He was a strong disciplinarian, and he was also an alcoholic. Those of you familiar with alcoholics know the kind of life you live. It is survival more than living. You learn to fear, not to trust, not to talk about your family life and never bring anyone home with you. You learn that love hurts. My father, on his death bed, regretted the lack of love. He said, "This is a house without love."
>
> (Wise One): Mix in the alcoholic and you have the physical and mental abuse, a good amount of rejection and a very unhappy life. Lina spent the rest of her life trying to make up for the lack of love.

(Dr. H.): Physical abuse is mentioned several times in Lina's background, but none clearly reported by her or any other Alter. There is an abundance of threats. We know that the threat, explicit or not, is many times more damaging that the act of aggression. "Damnum absque injuria" (damage without injury) was not the case with Lina. Lina attempted to describe and understand her mother.

> Then there is Mom. How should I describe her? Controlling, domineering, reserved (?) and so strong. Mom is a very sick woman. She spent years living with a man who was physically and mentally abusive. How proud she is that she kept the family together, yet she has an older son who she let her sister adopt. The marriage to my father was her second.
>
> She was raised in a little town in Tennessee with nine other brothers and sisters. I wonder what made Mom become the person she is. She had a lot of sickness

> when we were growing up: blood clot on her brain, cancer of the uterus, stroke. She was raped, beaten and left for dead. As you learn, the "others" have very little pity for this woman.

(Dr. H.): According to the experts and research done with patients showing personality disorders, it has been found that emotional, physical trauma(s) received by persons mainly from age two up to six, are the basis for provoking or triggering drastic changes in the frame of mind and personality of some susceptible persons. Continued trauma years after, will add more problems and reinforce the damage already in existence.

Lina refers to her Alters as the "Others"; they are the personalities that surface to meet me — to advise, quarrel, complain, and tell me about the events in Lina's life.

I could have used hypnosis to obtain more information, but in hypnotherapy the subject is induced, with his or her cooperation, to a regressive stage or time of their life in which they have a vivid recall of every minimal detail of what happened. They remember colors, smells, etc. I decided not to use hypnotherapy on Lina to prevent her recollection of old traumas with actual vivid distress. It would have been another traumatic experience with all of the anguishing fear and horror felt in the early years of her life. Another technical aspect of hypnosis is that the subject under hypnosis will remember what they "think" or believed happened, which may or may not reflect the factual reality. That is why, in Court, testimony under hypnosis is not accepted as legal evidence.

I also discarded the use of what is known as "truth serum," or the sodium amytal interview, which involves asking questions to the individual while injecting in the vein progressive doses of a type of barbiturate. The individual will remember and/or "open up," and answers questions. Again, the nightmare may become vivid with all the agony and suffering first experienced. This technique is known as "abreaction" — an episode of emotional release or catharsis associated with bringing into conscious recollection previously repressed unpleasant experiences.

I did not need to use those methods, since the Alters were cooperating. They knew what had happened. Most of them were "there" and little by little they were communicating with me and telling me what I needed to know. I did not need to enter into every minute detail. Knowing the main facts and the timeline was enough.

Someone reviewing this book, told me, "At times, it seems that the history of Lina goes back and forth." Some Alters told me the same things happening in the past life of Lina at different times during therapy. I have tried to avoid duplication of facts as much as possible, but at the same time, I did not want to eliminate it completely. It was not my history; it was theirs.

Lina continued writing, and the Wise One continued to take over, commenting on Lina's attempts to remember and understand what had happened to her.

> (Lina): I have an older sister with so many mental problems that she cannot function. It seems that the past is haunting her. She is really disabled. My youngest sister has no problems, according to her. She remembers what it was like, but chooses to forget, so she can go on living.

(Dr. H.): In regard to Lina's sisters, one of them is mentally crippled. She has received countless different "medicines for nerves," from different doctors. The other sister goes through life with an "I don't care" attitude. It seems as if she's living in a vacuum.

The first question I have yet to find a satisfactory answer to is when or what caused the first split for Lina. As best as I can figure, the oldest Alter is about forty. I don't know if it is forty years old, or it is the Alter's idea of being forty. Still I am searching.

> (Wise One): Those memories are behind the Wall, sealed forever, we all hope. The memories that have escaped are bad enough. She needed someone, and so we came. You cannot feel someone else's pain, nor can you judge how some would react to it. Even in our memories of this time, we see no faces, only hands...There was the "H———" family and the "Church." The "H——'s" were horrible people. They enjoyed torturing the helpless, and children are easy prey. Just the name of "H——" causes a tremendous amount of fear that Lina does not understand. There is also the "Church," where she sees shadows and someone dragging her. It is dark. It is night, in the middle of a cornfield. There is a huge flat stone. She is forced to sit there almost naked. Oh God, it is so cold! How much longer will this torture last? Why won't someone, anyone, stop this madness? We cannot let those memories come through.

(Dr. H): It seems that the "H—" family was living close to Lina's house and apparently, Lina's mother had a close or "friendly" relationship with them. The first time that the name of the "H——-" family was mentioned in my office, Lina became so agitated and began shaking so intensely that it seemed the whole office was trembling. She seemed to be experiencing fear and distress, so much so that she was sweating and complaining of pain in her arms, neck and legs. It was really pitiful. She was crying and repeating, "No, no, please don't." So much fear... So much distress... It was like some unknown force within her was torturing her.

Those pains were closely related to the early sexual trauma, which started as early as four years of age. I never entered into details, but I presume, it was a brutal abuse.

Lina is very intelligent. She developed a good rapport with me, and was able to develop acceptable insight rapidly, and that helped. Eventually, the psychotherapy lessened her body's discomfort and gradually it disappeared.

I would like to describe some of Lina's physical complaints or problems, as seen by her family physician, who happened to be my friend. He knew that I was treating her husband, who was also his patient, but he didn't know that I was treating Lina.

One day, he and I were having lunch together at the hospital, and I asked him about Lina's husband, Allen. His answer was, "He is happy to be seeing you. He is doing fine, but his wife is driving me crazy."

"Driving you crazy? Why," I asked?

"She is not always the same," he said.

I asked him what he meant by that.

"The other day she came in complaining of some abdominal distress. I examined her, and I felt a tumor or some localized hardening on one side of her abdomen. When she returned the next day, the complaints and the tumor were gone. Things like that have gone on for a long time. Today she has a problem, but tomorrow it is gone."

He told me that she was constantly complaining of tension in the back of her head, pain in her legs, shoulders, and so on.

He continued, "I started treating her six years ago, shortly after she married Allen. She needs you. She needs a shrink. Her blood pressure is a yo-yo. It is high for several days, but in the next visit, it is normal without medications." I did not tell him that she was already my patient.

In the late 1940s or early 1950s, an Austrian endocrinologist in Canada published a book, called *The Stress of Life,* which deals with the adaptation syndrome and describes the daily struggle for life. When a threat, either real or imagined, is perceived by a living organism, a decision has to be made to "fight or flight" in order to survive and preserve the integrity of the individual. This decision, most of the time, is subconscious. This almost daily struggle leads to physical distress with cardiovascular, gastrointestinal, and another symptoms, as well as emotional and mental problems. Symptoms provoked by our mind are called psychosomatic. The concept of psychosomatic medicine was not new to me. It was a part of my training as a neurologist and as a psychiatrist. That term is not used frequently today, but what other name could I use to explain Lina's body discomfort?

> The Wise One continued typing and providing information: How do we get her to understand they cannot hurt her anymore. They cannot scare her anymore. Even if they could, we would not allow it. As of today, Lina can endure great pain thanks to the No One. We have helped numb her body against physical pain.

(Dr. H.): I don't know who "they" were that were mentioned by the Wise One. The No One has been described as a powerful Alter or Personality full of hatred, anger, strength and adrenaline — potentially destructive and homicidal.

> (Wise One): We must explain all that happened in this period of her life. Her father was in Korea. War was going on. He was coming home on leave. Lina was waiting, hoping that he somehow would stop the pain. Wasn't he her daddy? Wouldn't he protect her? Didn't she sleep with his picture under her pillow? Didn't she ask God to send the one who smiles so lovingly at her from his picture? Surely he must love her.

(Dr. H.): Honoring Lina's confidentiality, I cannot be too explicit, but in trying to understand the best we can about the many drastic changes in Lina 's father, I need to mention an event in the life of this man. It was war time and her father was given permission to come home from abroad because of his wife's illness. While he was in the U.S., his unit was wiped out in combat in Korea. He was the only survivor. We don't know how much, how deep, how often this man was exposed to life-threatening situations. Today we are aware of the concept of Post Traumatic Stress Disorder and the deep emotional distress that characterizes this condition, with manifestations of nightmares, severe headaches, alcohol abuse, drastic changes in the personality and social interaction, withdrawal, violence, distrust, resentfulness, and guilt based on the question, "Why am I alive while so many around me were killed?"

> (Wise One): He was drinking heavily. He was an alcoholic. How could Lina, at that age, understand the workings of an alcoholic? Her so-called "uncles," friends of her mother, were not like this. How could she understand the workings of a mother who was lonely and who received Christmas cards from her husband's girlfriend? She remembered waiting and waiting and waiting. He was late. Why was Mother so afraid? Lina felt the fear in the air. Why should they be afraid? Wasn't this her daddy coming home? Then the cab pulled up to the door.
>
> Lina is remembering. She is not fighting the memories anymore. Lina is learning to trust us to allow us to help her. For so long we have only survived, now we must learn to live.
>
> Lina has tears. For once, she cries. Mass confusion sets in, but old memories and actual feelings slowly have started to become painful reality in her mind.
>
> This could not be her daddy; this is not the man in the picture. He looks like him. He has the uniform. He has the blue eyes, but not the warm, loving face. This one is acting funny; his words are cruel and slurred. His walk is unsteady. His blue eyes are not laughing; they are full of anger...Who is this man?
>
> Lina runs to him, wanting to hug him, wanting to find that warm smile. How could Lina understand? She couldn't. Her mother is crying. Her father is hit-

ting her. Lina's older sister is hiding. The younger sister is yelling, "Yes, Daddy, hit her, hit her again." Lina stood in the hallway and her mind was screaming. She cannot comprehend so much pain. The disappointment, the confusion was too much. She could not stay. She left. You wonder where she went. She came to us. Then he added, "This and more has gone on since she came to see me."

Some doubt the creation of us, even Dr. H. at the beginning. Unless you open your mind, you will never believe or understand. Do not some of you blindly believe in God? Have you not heard of the great acts done out of fear, panic, love? Have you not heard of the power of the mind? The remarkable powers of one's own will, the will of survival? The strongest force in any living creature is that of survival. Don't people go to great lengths to survive, so why not us and not a so-called Supreme Being, the so-called all-living, all-giving God who Lina prayed to. The one she begged to help her. The one she asked many times, "What have I done to suffer so?" The one Lina begged to forgive her for her so-called sins. What does a child of four have to beg forgiveness for? What sins could she have committed that her God would desert her in her time of greatest need?

The Preacher yells, "Those who commit sins against God will burn in everlasting Hell." Lina fears his words. She fears he can see her so-called sins. She crawls under the pews to hide herself. She runs to the outhouse to escape his condemnation, for he knows her sins, doesn't he?

Lina is bad, so bad... doesn't her mother tell her that? Lina doesn't understand what she has done that was so bad that He (God) would desert her. Lina needs someone to love her. Isn't there anyone who loves her, who wants her? Yes, but *he is bad*, he does bad things and she is bad for letting him. He plays GAMES with her. It hurts sometimes, but at least there is someone. Is that so bad? Yes! It is a sin; all of it is sinful. Lina does not understand; how could she? So she plays the GAMES.

(Dr. H.): When Lina writes, *"He is bad,"* she is talking about the one she calls "No Toe," who is a man from the "H—-" family, who frequently abused her sexually. I think that more than one person took advantage of her.

It seems that most of those sexual "games" occurred at the Pig House. I have already described early in therapy, Lynny Sue's reaction when, while she was drawing what appeared to be a house, I asked her if that was "the Pig House," and that question unleashed terror and a tremendous amount of fear. Terror, tears, anguish, sadness are poor words to describe what little Lynny Sue was showing. In that moment, her voice sounded like a very little, very fragile young girl.

(Wise One): Is there anything more innocent than a child? A child trusts so easily. So how does a child know, how does she understand that not all adults are good? How could she understand the games in the Pig House were not her sin, but his? How could she understand that everyone has a basic need to be touched and to feel loved? Lina knows of one memory of the Pig House and she fights us as we type. How strange that she still feels shame.

Dr. H. keeps telling her to get angry; instead she feels shame. Still she has trouble with anger. She feels guilty for participating in his games. Why can't she feel anger over what this one did? Why doesn't she feel violated by this one's acts?

Again, we must understand that she was a child, a child that felt neglected, unloved, and unwanted. A child, that one way or another, had been hurt, used,

> and frightened by every adult she had come into contact with, a child who learned to fear all adults, a child who learned not to trust any adults, a child who in the middle of all this, had found someone who wanted her. So this child took on the responsibility for someone else's sins, and continued her whole life to take the sins of others as hers, and through the She, to punish herself for them.

(Dr. H.): I feel that I need to explain again that every time Lina brought those papers for me to read, I would ask questions or make comments to clarify statements or to inquire more about some event. Those questions and commentaries were answered either by Lina herself or by one of the Alters. They were coming to the surface more often, sometimes by their own will, and other times at my request.

In answer to one of my questions, she gave me the full name of the man who was originally named the No Toe, and she gave me the exact location of the Pig House. What happened inside that place was of a heavy sexually abusive nature. I did not enter into a detailed description of facts, but her participation was basically passive based upon fear, and a great majority of the time it was imposed upon her. The No Toe abused Lina many times. He forced her to perform sexual acts that unleashed the horrible nightmares, confusion, and turmoil that she had been going through almost all the years of her life.

A couple of months before therapy ended, I asked her if she was feeling strong enough to go with her husband to the area where most of the sexual abuse happened. She refused. I did not insist. Up to that moment, I was not sure if she could hold the improvement already accomplished.

Her husband never knew every detail of what happened to her. He did not need to know. According to one of the Alters, Lina's husband's sexual behavior brought forth old memories hidden behind the Wall, triggering at one time so much distress, that it led to think of killing him.

I wondered what happened with Lina's grandfather. He loved her. She trusted him. They were very close. Why didn't she go to him at that time? It appears to me, that he detached himself little by little, and at the end, she felt completely abandoned by him. Many corners of Lina's past life were not clarified. Yet therapy was aimed at integration, and that was accomplished successfully by the end.

CHAPTER EIGHT

THE PROTECTORS. THE SHE. THE CORE

(Wise One): Lynny Sue came around age six, but decided at age seven that she wasn't going to grow up. She could not stand the touch of another human being. When asked why, she merely tells you that it hurts to be touched. Lynny Sue hates the four year old because she is dammed and will go to Hell.

You wonder, why Lina didn't tell someone. I ask you, how was she to know what to tell? How could a child at age four understand sexual abuse? How could she know that what he did was wrong? Was she not told to go ahead and tell; that no one would believe her anyway? When she did finally tell, he was right; no one believed her.

The memory is not clear to me for it is not mine: There was a tub, big and shiny. It was in the kitchen. The mother and some other woman were there ...no faces... Lina is standing in the wash tub, her mother is laughing. Lina is trying to explain. Her mother is saying, "Come on, tell me what he did to you?" All

Lina could hear was the laughter, all she could feel was confusion and the words, "Go ahead and tell, they won't believe you," echoing through her mind. He was right. But the No One did believe her.

Somewhere from deep within Lina we came. This was our beginning, the beginning of the Protectors. The She is one of us. Lina learned at an early age that sick people got attention. If someone cried loud enough or screamed hard enough there would be a reaction.

Lina could not handle the guilt associated with the Pig House. She could not handle guilt in association with acting up. So the She found she could use all these feelings as well as the need to punish Lina for all her bad behavior. Lina craved attention. She needed, more than wanted, love. Don't we all need to be loved? Even though the rejection was not intentional, Lina could only feel rejected. The She not only saw that Lina got attention, but also punished Lina for all the bad things causing the guilty feelings. Lina still carries many of the scars from those earlier attempts at self-destruction. The She would intentionally cut Lina. The She would inflict cigarette burns.

One incident that the Lady really resents is the scar on her right leg. Lina was living at a housing project on the Army Base at Fort Dix, New Jersey. There were some old buildings there; the floors were rotten. The She forced Lina's leg through the floorboard. The result was a laceration six inches long.

The She, in a way, is the most dangerous of us all. We keep her well protected away from the outside world for she has tried, and would destroy us all. Many times, at least five, the She has tried to kill herself (and us along with her).

> We rarely thought of our beginning. Where did we come from? How old are we? These were not important questions to our survival. As mentioned before, we do not have a concept of time. Our purpose, our goal, our reason for being is to keep the Core safe.
>
> We are, each in our own way, Protectors. Without the Core, we cannot exist. What is the Core? How can we explain to make you understand? It goes back to the original question. Where, at what point did the original split occur? At what point did Lina Y. [her name before she married Allen] decide she couldn't take it anymore? At what point did Lina Y. cease to exist? The original Lina Y. that came into the world on December 11, 1951, is the Core. You can say that Lina wished us into life. Lina was full of feelings she did not understand .She became so disillusioned with the real world that she decided she could no longer function in it. She slowly retreated from reality.

(Dr. H.): We need to understand that whatever is described, splitting, alters, and personalities, has nothing to do with Lina's volition or purposeful motivation. It was like a "mechanism of defense" within the person, a dissociation, in which the common denominator is the involuntary denial of the reality. MPD is actually called Dissociative Identity Disorder in the Diagnostic Criteria from DSM-IV.

> (Wise One): Which event caused Lina to "create" the Guardian to protect her, the Guardian to love her, the Guardian to watch over her soul? For that is what the Core is; the Core is Lina Y.'s soul, the one thing to which we all are connected. Within that cocoon lies a very battered soul, no longer suffering from the pain of a world she does not understand. Safe from a world that has offered her nothing but pain. Within our house reside seven children. The four year old

Lina who sits in a corner with her fingers in her mouth and never talks. Lynny Sue is there also. The events described all happened before age four, with the exception of the No One mentioning the mother's hospitalization and the fear instilled by the people in white. It is true that abuse started before age four, but it continued for many years after. So when the mother laughed at her, it shattered what little was left of Lina into pieces. These pieces became us.

In the beginning, there were just the Guardians and the No One. There were two Guardians. The Female is gentle, looking like a fairy godmother with long blond hair, blue eyes, all dressed in white with a warm and loving smile. The Male Guardian resembles an ogre, with long hair covering his whole body. He is fierce when needed to be, yet he has just a hint of gentleness when he tends to the Core. And of course, the No One is Lina's anger and hate.

The Guardians took Lina's essence, her soul at that time. They would not allow anyone or anything to ever harm her again. Amid the pieces, there was the anger, the guilt, the shame, the confusion, and the pain. Besides the feelings, there were also the memories. The combination of the two caused the destruction of Lina Y. It was decided that the two, memories and feelings, would never be allowed to meet again.

So they built a wall in the deepest part of Lina's mind. Each memory and feeling was sealed within a stone wall. It was decided that someone was needed to ensure that the Wall remained intact and that all feelings and memories that could cause harm were put into the vast blackness behind it. Hence the Gatekeeper was created.

> We are allowed knowledge of some past events, but not the actual memory or feeling. Sometimes the Gatekeeper allows the actual memory or feeling to form if needed for protection. At times, outside forces can be so strong as to overwhelm even the Gatekeeper and memory-feelings will come through; this can cause much damage.
>
> (No One): The force behind the Wall combined with one or more of us can cause mass destruction or great harm to ourselves or the person causing the disturbance.

(Dr. H.): While I was reading and reviewing this writing, I asked Lina, "Who wrote this?" This question was followed by a drastic change on Lina's face and with a deep tone of voice the answer came, "I did."

"You are the No One; you are very familiar to me," I said. No answer came from Lina, or from the No One.

I continued, "I'm taking this statement as information you are all giving me, but if somebody else reads it, not knowing what's going on, it can be taken as a threat." No answer either to that statement.

Again, I was glad we contracted "therapy without violence." I knew that I was not going to provoke a disturbance, but "they" were capable at the beginning, to distort communication or information requested and unleash destructive behavior.

If we consider that MPD is a consequence of early trauma in life, it may be called a sort of PTSD (Post Traumatic Stress Disorder) outcome. Along with this, a high incidence of comorbidity, with two or more problems at the same time, has been reported. If that is so, many patients who have reported having enhanced arousal sensitivity or overreaction to external stimuli, such as a friendly slap on the back, a sudden noise, or an innocent commentary, could be interpreting these actions as threats. Such people are in a chronic stage of readiness for fright reaction, and their response is unpredictable. In short, it is not what you say or what you do; it is their reaction to what they think you have said or done.

> (Wise One): We have already mentioned the She and the No One. The No One is very powerful for he has the original anger. Dr. H. once asked why Alters or Personality males were created, for lack of a better word. Were not males responsible for most of the pain? Indeed, great pain and guilt was caused by them. We are dealing with a child's mind, a child's perception and who could protect her better than a strong male?
>
> The No One is the ultimate protector. He will and can do anything to ensure the survival of the Core. He not only carries the anger; he also carries the hate. He has no compassion, no conscience. This is the Alter to fear. He can and has combined with the Male Guardian to become even more dangerous when the Core is threatened.

(Dr. H.): The Angry One is a split from the No One. This split was "needed" in order to be able to be "angry" without unleashing destructiveness.

> (Wise One): The Male Guardian is the only one who can keep the No One under control. We are always careful of the No One. He is the master of the Game. The Game to us is very real. In essence, it is survival, a Game without rules.

(Dr. H.): The format or context of the writing drastically changes here. When Lina brought those pages to review them with me, I asked her who wrote this part. She took the papers in her hands, and her voice and attitude changed drastically. She continued reading what was typed, shouting at the top of her [his] lungs. "I care nothing for the others! You need me. I am the No One." From there on, he repeated, "You need me! Without me, you would be nothing. I'm not weak. Without me you would not survive! I care nothing for the feelings of the mother. I don't care that the father is finally rotting in a grave. My satisfaction was in watching his living in hell and how much he suffered his last five years of life!"

(Dr. H.): Lina's father was in and out of hospitals many times, and was very sick until he died.

> (This angry male voice continued shouting):"How dare he mourn the lack of love when he failed so badly in the giving! How I hate Lina for caring for them. What did either of them ever do for her? Did they ever care for her suffering? No, her feelings were silly, stupid. How many beatings must a person take? How much cruelty must one human being take before they are grateful for the clothes on their back? Where was the love for her? Where was there ever kindness shown to her? They must pay for all they have done! All who has harmed her must pay! Vengeance is mine, says the Lord. Bullshit! It belongs to me. I will extract my pound of flesh."

(Dr. H.): As I said before, this is the No One talking. How much hate he had. He even hated Lina for what she took, and yet he was created to protect her. What a contradiction! How can you hate the same one you care for so much?

When Lina and I were discussing the previous passages in therapy, I addressed what follows to the No One. I told him, "In your anger and hate, you have become blind. You want to protect the Core. You know that the Core is Lina, so you want to protect Lina. You brag about being so powerful. You and the 'Others' have blocked memories and feelings. Now you all demand that she should react to memories that either she doesn't have or are not clear or are distorted."

There was no answer from the No One.

I continued, "Your approach is to reassure yourself that you are strong and powerful, but you fail to realize that you are as strong and powerful as the Core can be. You must stop that shouting and your threatening attitude. It will alienate you with people who care, people who are willing to help. At first I was concerned. I was not afraid of you, because I knew that you cared, but you have to start thinking about how to be more civil."

Again, there was no answer. Lina appeared to be sad. She was very quiet. I asked her, "Are you aware of what is going on"?

She tilted her head and in a very soft tone of voice, said, "Some."

The reading of the notes continued. This time the Wise One was in charge again.

> (Wise One): This is not nor will it be the story of Lina's life.

(Dr. H.): "If not, then what is it?"

> (Wise One): Parts are sealed off and should stay that way. Lina must learn to deal with life. We give only what she needs in order to do that. She must accept her life as it was and not as the fairy tale we let her create. We accept that we are responsible for some of the turmoil in her life. Lina has suffered because of us, but she must understand she could not have survived to this point in her life without us.
>
> The She is the only threat to the Core, for not even the No One would harm the Core. Only when Lina understands the She, the part that the She has in her life, then the "need" of the She will be removed, and we can give the She the peace she so deserves.

(Dr. H.): This response was very good. The Alters were learning that some of them may be not be needed anymore. Lina was learning about her past; memories and feelings were entangling. More and more she was in charge without the need to escape and, consequently, no other personality taking over.

People have the right to be angry. People should be assertive. It was nice to be wise, meaning that some of the personalities were welcome to stay with Lina, but only as long as she was in charge and in control. It would be nice to have an assertive, but non-destructive No One around.

The Alters were helping me to help Lina regain control of herself and take responsibility for her actions and decisions. It seems to me that my therapy was showing some positive results, and regarding interactions with the Alters, the Angry One was fading away more and more.

The Wise One helped me tremendously. Sometimes, I felt he was the one conducting the therapy.

The No One became more cooperative and less vociferous. I have not reported every word he said, since he spoke like a "carretonero," which is Spanish for a person who uses one filthy word for every three words he speaks.

Now Lynny Sue accepted Lina and the four year old as part of herself. The Woman, The Lady. and the Bitch were merging with Lina, with the Lady leading the group. More and more Lina was coming for therapy better dressed, not so inhibited, and smiling more often.

CHAPTER NINE

FLASHES OF BAD CHILDHOOD MEMORIES. RECOLLECTION OF A FIRST MARRIAGE AND HER THREE CHILDREN'S INFANCIES

(Wise One): Lina has suffered from headaches since the age of nine. Every time she was taken to the doctor, she was told there was no physical reason for them. The so-called doctors told her mother that Lina just wanted attention. Yes, she did, but she was not making up the pain.

Lina, to this day, still fears doctors and hospitals. She learned early not to trust. How could she when fear was so deeply instilled in her subconscious? She was told to behave and quiet down or a doctor would come with a big needle and give her something to calm her down.

Lina is now remembering the hallway; the smell of the hospital to her was a smell of fear and death. Lina's sisters are there. We are all sitting on chairs hooked together. We are all dressed up. I only get a glimpse of hands. Strange. It seems that every time the mother went away to that place with those people, she came back different. Lina still cannot deal with people leaving. How she suffered when her oldest son, Billy, left home. The separation was unbearable; she still grieves over the loss of the bond between them.

After Lina married Allen, her second husband, he started making negative remarks about her family. It was so often, that her oldest son decided to go to the West Coast, and shortly after, he joined the Navy. Lina's three grown children are from her first marriage. One child was stillborn.

Rowdy [name of a personality] took over Lina's teenage years. Rowdy was wild, and as a consequence, she became pregnant. The man she was going with at that time married her. She has little memory of her first marriage. She knows she has three grown boys, but most of the time she cannot even remember how old they are. Just recently, with the help of therapy, she had her first memory of them when they were small.

We have mentioned a few personalities, splits or Alters of the children. The Core Lina is four years old. Lynny Sue, who is six, and Lizzy, about five, came to help with laughter. This was the time when the uncles [mother's friends?] were around more. It was Lizzy who came when Lina could not stay during the night of her father's return. Everyone liked to laugh. Poor Lizzy tried to find happiness through laugher. Doesn't everyone love a clown? She does not laugh anymore. Laughter could not survive in the face of fear.

A babysitter [someone from the H.... family] thought it was funny to scare children. She would tell stories, and her boyfriend would stalk around the house, making faces in the window and then disappear. Perhaps it was harmless fun to an adult, but not to a child hiding under a chair, shaking. Lina was a very sensitive child.

The Bitch once told Dr. H. that Lina would believe anything she was told. She believed that if she ate a watermelon seed, it would grow into a watermelon in her belly. Lina believed that every time she got a bump on her tongue, it was because she told a lie, and she would agonize over the lie she told. Lina was too afraid of adults not to believe everything they said. Lizzie just stopped laughing one day.

Then there was Lonnie, a tomboy who sought to be alone. She spent all her time in the field of wildflowers behind the house. Lonnie would swing on vines, climb trees, and enjoy the quiet of the woods. Lonnie did not need anyone. She had her own dog, Bouncy. Bouncy was a Dalmatian, and she belong to Lonnie. Bouncy was all she needed. Bouncy didn't mind that Lina wet the bed. Bouncy had her puppies in Lonnie's bed. Oh boy! Was her mother mad about Bouncy tearing up the mattress!

"What happened to the puppies?" Lina asked, after hearing the cries from under the house? NO, it couldn't be. How could all the puppies crawl under the house and fall in the old cistern? Please, someone help them. Oh God, please! The sound, the yelping, it seemed like it would never stop. There wasn't anything anybody could do to get them out. Why?

Then Bouncy was gone, and so was Lonnie. Bouncy was hit by a car. Lonnie tried to go to Bouncy. The mother wouldn't let Lonnie go into the road. The car did not see Bouncy, but Lonnie saw the car. Lonnie wanted to go with Bouncy. Bouncy was the only one who loved her. Didn't her mother understand? Yes, her mother understood, "Don't be so stupid. It was just a dog, just a stupid dog."

Lynn [Lynny Sue] came. Such a sweet child who tells you that her mother loves her, not like Lina's mother. Lynny Sue hates the four year old. She is damned and is going to hell, but not Lynny Sue. She is a good girl. She likes to draw. She is very creative. Lynny Sue came at age six, and at age seven decided she was not going to be a grownup. She would not become one of them. She fears all adults. She was afraid to even talk to them, but she loves to play. Her mother showed her how to make doll furniture out of cereal boxes. She had a doll, a Betsy Wetsy, her favorite. It got burnt up in a fire.

The memory is foggy, not clear. School was a terror to all of us. The fear of adults was so instilled in our memory. The No One could not be allowed to deal with the real world, we soon learned. He was too angry, too strong. Lina became known for her "temper." The No One learned the power of fear, and so he used it. He realized his full potential. He has inflicted great harm to other people. He attacked Lina's first grade teacher. Lina was no good at math. We tried to help, but she just got more confused. The No One blamed her teacher. Lina did not wish to go to school anymore. The teacher was grabbing her and dragging her into class. This was not allowed. No one would hurt her again, no one would force her. No one would ever be allowed to threaten her again. We all felt the panic. Who did she think she was? What an old bitty. Instead of trying to help, she made us sit in the corner wearing a dunce hat. Lina could not take the shame.

Lina's terror of adults was so strong that in the second grade she peed in her pants in front of the whole classroom, as she stood by the blackboard. She had been too afraid to ask permission to go to the bathroom.

(Dr. H.): What follows still is one of the Protectors writing, perhaps the Wise One, but here they are trying to explain their presence. Also, they are showing some conflictive feelings within themselves and within Lina.

(Wise One?): Lina's family moved a lot because of her father's need to go from one military post to another. Lina lost many friends and soon learned not to make any more, withdrawing more and more into us.

As protective as the No One is of the children, sometimes he acts like he hates the Lina of today.

The Bitch questions why Lina should be in control, "Isn't she the weakest link in the chain?"

We constantly question ourselves. As a child, Lina needed us to survive, to deal with a world she could not understand. Today she is an adult, and with the help of Dr. H., she is becoming more and more aware of us and learning how to deal with this world. We have decided to promote deepening that awareness. She still needs us, although at times, it seems we may be adding more problems.

Have we gone too far in that protection? Maybe if the abuse had stayed in the past, but in Lina's life there was much more to come. As traumatic as sexual abuse is, Lina may have been able to deal with that alone, but she also had an alcoholic father. She suffered physical and mental abuse. There was the constant moving, with her father leaving and coming back and the mother sick and abusive and gone most of the time. There was the hell and damnation preacher, and the H... family, and more to come.

> In Lina's home, there were many secrets. She was told, "Don't tell anyone. What goes on in our home is nobody's business."

(Dr. H.): I saw Lina's mother one day in my office in the waiting room. I do not remember why she came, but I do remember her. She tried to be flamboyant and was ridiculous. Her behavior was very inappropriate and I felt really sorry that Lina had to deal with a person like that.

CHAPTER TEN

LINA WANTED TO DIE. THE TANK PRECEDED THE NO ONE. ROWDY TAKES OVER. THE NO ONE'S HOMICIDAL INTENT.

(Dr. H.): The Wise One continued writing, and although he appeared to be repetitive, he was giving more and more information of the past. Indeed, the details were fragmented, but it was like a puzzle, in which the pieces are put together one by one and slowly take form.

> (Wise One): Lina felt empty, unwanted, unloved. She would do anything to get a kind word. She craved someone to hold her, to love her, even to like her. Yet she feared the touch of others. When someone got close, they seemed to want something. What price would she have to pay for the kindness? In the past, the price had been too high.
>
> Lina's mother would ask her what happened to her, "Skinny Lynny. You used to be so skinny." Lina sought solace in food. Lina became fat, and, therefore, unac-

ceptable. She was teased and made fun of, so she withdrew even more.

At the age of fourteen, she would lay awake at night and pray, "If there is a God, please don't let me wake up tomorrow." She even made a deal with God. "If I am good until I'm sixteen, please don't let me live beyond my sixteenth birthday." Lina felt empty. Fear and pain were constant.

Something happened one day. The memory is foggy. Lina tried several times to kill herself by OD [over-dose], once with Darvon and another time she almost died taking the sleeping pills her father used. The mother couldn't understand what happened to her "good girl."

More pain, more frustrations. Lina's younger sister was 12. Lina was 13, and her older sister was 15. The 12 year old sister tried to overdose with sleeping pills. Lina found her in the bathtub barely coherent. Lina called her mother at work.

"Give her coffee and walk her around," the mother said. "I will be there when I can."

Lina got her older sister to help. Mother finally arrived. Lina didn't know where her father was. Her mother was angry, saying her little sister only wanted attention. Lina wanted to call an ambulance.

"Oh, no," said her mother! "The neighbors, the police, we can't have that."

They drove her to a hospital, forty-five minutes away. Lina was afraid they wouldn't make it in time.

Why was the mother more worried about what the neighbors thought than the life of her daughter? This was not right, something was very wrong here. Mothers weren't supposed to be like that.

Lina could not keep her deal with God. One night as she laid crying and looking out the window, the pain and the loneliness overwhelmed her. She escaped again and came home to us. Thus began Rowdy and ended the one we called Teen.

More memories: Rowdy and the No One would not let anyone push them around. There were constant fights with her mother and father. Rowdy wanted her driver's license, and her father was mad because her mother had hired Yellow Cab to teach her to drive. Lina was standing in front of the stairwell. Her father slammed his fist into Rowdy's face. Her father was hitting her; he was going to knock her down. Her father did not know who he was dealing with. Rowdy with the help of The No One got in a fist fight with him. Hell hath no fury like the No One. Once again, her mother took her father's side and Lina was once again an ungrateful, hateful daughter. Her mother was furious with Lina. How dare she hit her father! How could her mother justify what her father was doing to Lina? Her mother did not even try. Lina was just a terrible daughter for striking her father. By now Lina had heard over and over again, "Lina, you have changed. Lina, what has come over you? You were never like that before." The No One was in his glory. He was the "Tank," the bully of the neighborhood. Nobody was safe from his anger and aggressiveness. She went up to a weight of 263 pounds.

(Dr. H.): Because Lina was extremely heavy, she had gastric bypass surgery a few years before she came to see me, but her weight problem triggered further conflictive problems in her relationship with friends and mainly with her mother. Her mother did not let her enter her house from the front door. Her mother told her to use the rear door and avoid been seen by any neighbors. This overt rejection was during Lina's teenage years.

> (Wise One): Rowdy is unafraid of anything. She is everything Lina is not. She is fun-loving, outgoing. She makes friends, and people like her. She is a bit wild. She is the whore her mother accused Lina of being. Rowdy is now sixteen: she dances, she drinks, she lives, and she will not become an adult. She doesn't want the hassles or the responsibility of being an adult. Lina is afraid of people; Rowdy is not.

> (What follows seems to have been written by Rowdy): Dr. H. said that I'm not that important, but without me, Lina would never have any fun. Life without fun is a desolate place. Besides that, you need to be young in order to grow older.

(Dr. H): This statement gave me the impression that Rowdy still was around.

> (Lina): I know this jumps around a lot. This is easy for me to explain. There is more than one writing this. Each Alter has their own personality, each one with their own set of values, each one with their own fears. Most, until recently, were unaware that they are all part of the same person, that they are all connected to me, that they are a part of me. I will leave their writing as it is. Through their writings I have learned to understand them and accept them.

(Dr. H.): The previous statement from Lina shows that her therapy is going in the right direction. She has accepted her MPD problem. She is showing respect for the Alters without fear. She has started to take responsibility; "They are part of me."

> (Wise One): We began writing this as a suggestion from Dr. H. to help Lina record things she remembers between sessions with him, to basically find the parts missing from Lina's memory. It is very much like the last line in the nursery rhyme, "Humpty

Dumpty."— "All the King's horses and all the King's men could not put Humpty together again." Dr. H. is trying to put Lina back together again, and like the King's horses and the King's men, he will not be able to put Lina together again. We strive to all work together, but we will not leave. This is very much our fate.

(Dr. H.): At the beginning of therapy, and before that, every Personality or Alter thought of himself or herself as unique and independent. This last statement shows a sense of unity and their desire to cooperate with the therapy, but at the same time, it reflects their fear of disappearing completely and their ambivalent feelings regarding the outcome of the therapy.

(Wise One): The Guardian and I, (known as the Wise One) came to realize that we cannot all merely just survive. Lina must be able to live. There are some who still doubt. There are some who still fight the idea of one person being in control.

There are too many pieces to put back into one piece. Each piece has its own strengths. Some of the older ones are just too powerful to fit back into Lina. Yet, if we stay as we are, what are the alternatives? We agonize over this. Should we take back what we have already given? Should we continue with Dr. H.?

In the beginning, was it not our purpose to protect the Core so that Lina could survive and live? We came to take away the pain for Lina. We must all work together, now more than ever to help her. Do not misunderstand. We do not pity Lina or feel sorry for her. Life is hard. We did not create the situations in her life. We came when no one else would. We must strive to strengthen Lina so she will be able to look back into the shadows that scare her and see the light, so that she—for only Lina can—take down the stones of the Wall one by one and look at them without caus-

> ing destruction. She is not ready now and she may never be able to deal with them at all.

(Dr. H.): Again here we see the ambivalence of those powerful Alters; on one hand, they want to stay independent, but on the other, they would like to see Lina take over.

> (Wise One): Our fears are real; our doubts are real. The last time that the two worlds touched, there was so much destruction. Dr. H. still asks what happened to cause that much fear and destruction. There are no words to describe the depths of the emotion that erupted in that bedroom. This is another time, another place.

(Dr. H.): Later, I was told that four years ago, Lina had an outburst of violence and destruction which required police intervention.

Lina told me that the No One was driving a brand new car that Allen had just bought and tried to kill her husband, but ended crashing the car against a tree. The No One meant to kill him, although Lina's husband never knew that the car was aimed at him. Lina was committed to a psychiatric hospital after being subdued by force. She was the one driving the car, which had a stick shift. Lina doesn't know how to drive a car with a stick shift, not even today, after the therapy ended.

Some explanation for this horrible incident correlates to Lina's past victimization from sexual abuse that she was subjected to for many years, starting early in her life. I was told more than once, by the No One and also by the Wise One that her husband Allen was using and abusing sex in order to control her.

He would tell her over and over that, "No one else can make you feel so good." Every time she refused to have sex, he insisted more and more. One day was the "straw that broke the camel's back." Lina's No One needed to stop the repetition of sexual acts forced upon her. In the past, the abuse was against the Gentle One. This time, it was the powerful No One. He was there to defend her. He took over, this time with homicidal intent. The Gentle One disappeared shortly after Lina's second marriage.

CHAPTER ELEVEN

THE NIGHT IS DARK, THE STONE IS SO COLD.

(Dr. H.): We needed to deal with Lina's frequent flashbacks of feeling cold, of being threatened by darkness, her crippling fear of snakes, and other phobias, but we also needed to deal with her current family problems, because they were interfering with the healing process of past traumas. Lina's difficulties included dealing with her husband, her mother, her sisters, her three grown children, her granddaughter, Carla, and her father who was very sick and dying.

> (Wise One): We must decide the best way to deal with what is going on now. It is causing many problems for us. There have been many losses in Lina's life. The loss of Carla is very dangerous for us.

(Dr. H.): Carla is Lina's granddaughter. Carla's mother divorced Lina's oldest son and made plans to move to California. During psychotherapy, Lina tried to have some acceptance, but then she said, "Carla may feel abandoned, the way I felt." It was very painful for her to see her granddaughter taken away.

> (Wise One): We must keep a close watch on Lina. The possible separation from Carla is bringing feel-

ings never experienced before by Lina. These feeling are too new, too sharp, and Lina has not had the time we have had to deal with them. Lina feeds into the She, the She feeds into the No One. We must watch the situation.

Do we alert Dr. H. to what is going on or do we wait and hope that it will work itself out with only our help? Dr. H. understands how Lina is connected to Carla. Does he understand the amount of pain involved in this loss? Does he understand her fear of losing Carla? Does he understand that through the She, Lina feels she deserves this loss? Does he know how the She reminds Lina of what a "terrible" person she is, and how the She manipulates Lina into believing she deserves this punishment? The She says Lina is such a bad person. Lina so wishes to fight for her rights, and yet Lina feels she has no rights.

Lina has lost so much in her life. She allowed Carla to fill the void in her. Now she is gone, and we have to put Carla's things away, but Lina keeps bringing them back out. Lina cries, and with tears running down her face, she yells, "What have I done to deserve this?" Lina is grieving for her lost dreams. She longs for a close, loving family, but there is none. Those feelings of being alone disturb the Teen. The Teen understands how she feels. The Teen is very close to Lina, and the She is never far away. We watch as Lina suffers. Lina looks at her two younger sons and does not understand what went wrong. Even the oldest doesn't remember her birthday most of the time. When he comes "home," he stays at Grandma's because he is not comfortable with Lina's husband.

Lina's husband doesn't care much for him, nor for the other two, and that hurts Lina. Dreams to have a happy home filled with family, friends and love never

> came true. Dreams became a nightmare. Emptiness again, and Lina wonders if reality is worth all the pain.
>
> Dr. H.'s therapy aimed at helping Lina function on a reality basis and not on guilt or a distorted sense of duty. Lina's relationship with her mother is based on the later, and the result is tremendous ambivalence and confusion. It is so difficult to hate and to love, to accept and to reject, to feel close and distant— all at the same time, and that is reflected in her relationship with her mother. That's why Dr. H. wishes for Lina to break from her mother. We (the Personalities) wish this, too. Lina wishes this also and is trying very hard to accomplish this.

(Dr. H.): I did not really want to see Lina completely detached from her mother. My goal was to help her say no when requests from her mother were difficult, or required time or effort that she could not accomplish and which, consequently, triggered more guilty feelings. Her mother was impossible to please most of the time, and she was constantly asking Lina for things.

> (Wise One): The father, just before he went into surgery, had the daughters promise to take care of their mother. Of course, Lina promised. For the last ten years she has been taking care of both of them. How it hurts Lina to sit back and listen as her mother brags about how Lina's younger sister is taking care of her, to listen as her mother raves on and says she just doesn't know what she would have done without her good friends to help her, and not one word about the things Lina has done for her. Lina is beginning to feel anger toward her mother. Before, it was always the No One who personalized the anger. She is starting to resent her mother, starting to ask why she puts up with her.
>
> This feeling of anger is new for her, and she feels guilty. "Mother is sick." Lina is still that little girl

who craves a kind word or gesture from her parents. Still she seeks their approval. Lina was devoted to her father in his last years. He was helpless, and she was the only one who, no matter what, was there. The last year of his life, Lina was there before she went to work; she was there for lunch and after lunch. She was the only one her father trusted to take him to the VA Hospital for his appointments. She was constantly tired and worn out, but she was there. Finally after forty years, her father told her he loved her the best way he knew how. He had waited until he was dying to tell her that, and then she promised him that she would take care of her mother — how could she not keep her promise?

Lina knows how empty her mother's life seems. The grandchildren no longer go to see her mother. Her mother really has no one else. Lina knows how that feels to reach out and to find no one there. Can she do the same? Lina realizes she is not the kind, loving mother she has imaged, but a lonely, old woman. Shouldn't someone care? Lina has called her youngest sister for help. She just can't come. She has a job, etc. She sends some money for her mother every month. Lina cannot make her mother go to her sister. Lina finds herself feeling frustrated, angry, trapped. Trapped by feelings she is just beginning to feel and identify but not quite understand.

Lina gets glimpses of a dark, cold place. She has horrible feelings of being trapped. She doesn't understand the hives she gets when she takes a bath. A doctor told her mother that Lina was allergic to water [?], but the hives only cover the part of Lina's body that is out of the water.

(Dr. H.): There is one incident that happened to Lina while taking a bath. Her mother saw bruises on Lina's body. Lina tried to tell about the "predator" abusing her, but the outcome of that was her mother making fun of her.

Something strange happened to her one night in Tennessee in the early years of her life. It was a dark, cold night, and she was forced to sit and stay for long time on a big, flat stone in the middle of a corn field. I was told that this was a sort of religious ritual. We don't know how old she was, but she was very young. This incident was reported to me by the Alters more than once, but Lina herself could not give me further details. I never insisted on knowing more.

> (Wise One): Lina does not understand her insane fear of snakes. Just mention that one is near, and she stops dead in her tracks and starts screaming. Her "insane" fear is so strong that she cannot even tolerate looking at worms. Her mother explains that Lina's fear of snakes was caused by her, the mother. She says she was scared by a snake when she was carrying Lina. Lina knows that her older sister was bitten by a copperhead snake "while playing on the swing set in their backyard."

(Dr H): The No One told me about the snakes, and what the No One told me is not the same explanation as her mother's.

> (Wise One): Some years ago, Lina's family doctor sent her to a psychiatrist who wanted to hypnotize her to find out when and where that fear started, but he was just too expensive. The family couldn't afford him; they had no insurance. Then she started going for therapy at a community mental health center. There she started learning that not everyone was like her.

(Dr. H.): She didn't understand. Flashes of fragmented images appear to be detaching from "The Wall." The No One appeared to be more friendly and communicative with me and very much concerned about the possibility of Lina's falling apart upon knowing about this past time of her life. The Wise One was constantly surfacing and communicating to me his concern. It is difficult to know what Lina's reaction would be when those memories become accessible.

Going back to Lina's fear of snakes, it was a very valid fear and not a sort of neurotic reaction or symbolism in her mind. Her family spent a great part of her childhood in rural Kentucky and some time in rural Tennessee. I was told about a ritual for members of a Church that was held from time to time. It was a ritual of either acceptance and/or purification in which the person to be tested would be exposed to bodily contact with more than one snake, perhaps copperheads. The church members believed that the snakes would not bite or do harm if the person being tested was clean and free of sins.

At the beginning of this book, I mentioned that one of my co-therapists was experienced in treating people who had been exposed to satanic cult activity and the emotional distress this triggered years later. I was told by him and others later on, that in these types of rituals, children would be placed into a large box with rats or other animals such as snakes. This was out of the scope of my knowledge and I did not try to find out further the validity of this.

> (Wise One): The images, the feelings, the memories come from the Wall. Although they seem very old and powerful, the bricks appear not to be so silent and holding. Lina has become stronger, hopefully strong enough to handle the bricks.
>
> At this time in therapy, Lina was walking in two worlds, both very real for her, both filled with the unknown. She is a child and a woman at the same time, a mother, a daughter, a wife, and yet, she is us! She is fighting for survival every day, every second. At the same time, she craves an end to the pain. She is tired of the fights and yearns to rest, and end the shadows, the fear and the search. This is strengthening the She, and this is dangerous. We keep on watching and we constantly remind her that things will get better,

> things will work out. There is a light at the end of the darkness. She is asking, "What is happiness?" If there is no happiness, is there at least contentment? Are we offering empty promises? There is more to living than us. We must strive not to voice our doubts. Lina must not pick up on ours. She has enough of her own.
>
> (The writing that follows is done by Lina herself): There seems to be so much to deal with. I'm so tired. I sleep and yet feel my eyes have never closed. All I feel like doing is sleeping, and yet I must continue. It is so difficult to be in the here and now. Lately I have lost time again. That has not happened for long time. Where is this terrible feeling of apprehensive dread coming from? It seems to be coming from deep within. For what I have learned, the fear I'm feeling seems to be fear transmitted from the Gentle One. I know that Dr. H. wishes to communicate directly with her and she is fighting this.

(Dr. H.): When Lina brought this writing to review it with me, I asked her to tell me more about this almost new Personality (or was it a split?). What was the reluctance to communicate or to face me? A few weeks earlier, I was not looking at Lina directly. Then when I did look at her, her face changed dramatically. It was a face of serenity, smiling in a gentle manner; even her hair around her face was shining, as if it were flooded with some light — a very pleasant and peaceful image. At the risk of sounding ridiculous, I thought it was like looking at an angel. This lasted for a few seconds. What I saw was the face of a woman reflecting serenity, but she disappeared without telling me who she was. The session of therapy was over. Lina went home and promised to type more.

The next week, she brought what follows.

> (Wise One): The Gentle One wishes no contact with the outside world. She left, and the Shell took over. What caused this? I, the Wise One, will try once again

to fill in the gaps, so much to explain. The creation of the Shell was needed. She has the ability to draw in any information in any given situation without having any emotion of her own. In a way, she *was* a form of integration, for she could draw on any one or all of us depending upon the situation. That is how Lina's second husband detected us, even though he didn't understand exactly what was going on. The Shell did not have a real identity of her own, so therefore, he saw the No One, the Bitch, the Woman, the children, and at times, combinations of us.

The Shell doesn't have or show emotions, or at least emotions don't affect her. It was the Shell that the Core invested herself in to become "immune" to any external aggression, real or imagined. The purpose *was* to keep Lina sheltered. Lina could not deal with us and the world around her.

(Dr. H.): The italicized word above points out that whoever is typing, most probably the Wise One, is describing the Shell in past tense, as if she were nonexistent at the present time. Maybe the alters are feeling more confident and secure coming to the surface and communicating without the need to hide in a sort of transient split. I had not seen the "Feeler" or the "Doubter" either surfacing or mentioned anymore.

After over one year of therapy, I was feeling acceptably relaxed and confident working with "Them." Transference was well established and I felt that I was helping Lina.

CHAPTER TWELVE

ROWDY'S PREGNANCY. LINA'S MARRIAGES .

(Wise One): Lina weighed 263 pounds. Food was used for many years to try to fill the emptiness of her life. The Lady was at her constantly over her appearance, which later led to her having gastric by-pass surgery. [This is a surgical procedure performed on morbidly overweight patients to help them lose weight by reducing the capacity of the stomach.] The She was at her worse, reinforcing the Lady by telling her how fat she was, how she should feel ashamed by the way she looks.

Lina was in her early twenties at that time. Suicidal thinking was almost constant. She wanted to die. We couldn't stop Lina and the She when, a couple of times, we overdosed with Darvon and another time with 35 sleeping pills. The She even threw us down a flight of stairs, but we only cracked a couple of ribs that time.

After the suicide attempts, Lina was hospitalized in a psychiatric facility. She didn't know why she took the sleeping pills. She couldn't explain. She was "very tired." A big, fat doctor told her it was just a case of cabin fever. The No One did not like the doctor, so he threw her out of the room. After discharge, Lina attended group therapy, and later on, partial hospitalization for over two years, twice a week. We must remember that Rowdy was still around. She was not much interested in love, but did indulge in sex for enjoyment. For most of us, love was associated with pain, but Rowdy would not allow herself to be hurt. No one would interfere with her fun. She enjoyed life.

Lina found she was pregnant. She told the man and he said they would get married. Her mother had a fit. She did not like this man at all. Mother was not aware of the pregnancy. Lina found someone who wanted her and she would do anything to please him. She needed someone badly.

He loved her the best he could, but his father was also an alcoholic, so you have here two children of alcoholics together. The marriage was eight years old when Lina seemed to wake up and realize something was wrong. Lina did not love her first husband for she had no idea what love was. All she knew was that he wanted her. He said he loved her and that was what Lina craved, someone to love her. Lina's first husband knew nothing of us. He just ended up thinking Lina was crazy.

(Lina herself typed what follows): During this time, I thought I was going crazy. I would hear the kids. At least at that time I believed it was one of my children. Later, I realized it was me. I would hear them calling for help or just hear a little child calling for her mother, and I would go and look for them. I would go hysterical before I would realize that the boys were at school.

I was seeing shadows and thinking it was people trying to get me. I even believed that someone had put a bomb in my bathtub.

My oldest child, age five at that time, would have to call my mother. She found me many times hiding, terrified and not recognizing anyone. What those children went through at that time, I can only guess.

On another occasion, I knew I had bought some rice from the grocery and I couldn't find it. I ran around the house like a crazy person accusing the neighbors of stealing food from us. I found bacon in the linen closet and accused one of my children of trying to intentionally drive me crazy.

I finally went to see my family doctor and broke down and told him everything. He sent me to a psychiatrist, the one who wanted to use hypnosis, but we could not afford him. So much confusion and disorientation, my memory is failing.

(Wise One): Many times, the oldest child had to call someone to get Mommy out of the corner. Many times, the husband would call from work and have to rush home and care for her. Something had to be done, so many years in therapy, so many pills prescribed, so much group therapy.

But this time was not really wasted; we learned a lot. We learned that we could not continue the way we were, so we created the Gentle One. Lina needed a new start. She needed some softness, some kindness, some love in her life, so we drew from those around us. There was the caring of Donna, the humor of Brenda, the understanding from Ben, and we created the Gentle One, like people should be.

(Dr. H.): Those are the real names of some of the therapists involved at that time in Lina's treatment. Their involvement was very positive, and I believe they planted the seed of hope.

(Wise One): For the way people should be is not the way people really are. We created a personality who had no memory of the past hurts, the past rejections. She was so innocent, too innocent for this world. We created the Gentle One.

The divorce was final. Lina felt free for the first time in her life, but she did not know what to do with the freedom. Lina left the boys with their father. She could not care for them. She had no job and no place to go to but to her mother, and another year of school to finish. At the time, it seemed the best thing for the children. She did not wish to uproot them like she had been so many times before. She had no permanence in her childhood and wished that so much for her children. It would be better for them to stay in the only home they knew.

The ex-husband told the children that she was crazy. It wasn't hard to convince them that their mother had been running around on him and hanging out at bars. This was all untrue, but what did that matter? Lina had to let them go in order to get them back, and eventually she did. The middle boy was the one who blamed her for most of the abandonment. The children were with their father. This hurt, but she believed she had to let them go. If they truly loved her, they would come back.

Everyone loved the Gentle One. Lina was so good, too good to be true. She gave freely and asked for nothing in return. Of course, there was her husband, Allen; he also was too good to be true. He listened to her. He treated her with kindness. He was there for her when things got bad. He was her friend. He would be there when she needed to cry. She could tell him anything, and he wouldn't judge her. He just cared for her. For one brief, shining moment, there was a

Camelot, but Camelot was not real, and neither was he. She could not see what he really was. She looked at his face and saw a savior. He triggered a memory of a picture of Christ that her mother kept on the wall, such a kind, gentle face. He needed her; she would take care of him. She needed him. She could fix him.

We tried to warn her. We tried to get her to leave him. He was Jekyll and Hyde. She fought us. She would not let herself see him for what he was. When she did, it was too late. She believed everything he said. He tried to turn her against her mother and her children. He was constantly belittling her children. She was a "bad mother." On the other hand, his children were so perfect, and when his daughter misbehaved, it was from being around Lina's children. He would not allow Lina to have her children around when his children were there, which was almost every week for his daughter (his favorite?). He could not see how much his daughter hated Lina, nor the cold way his other children treated her. This was hard for the Gentle One to understand. She tried to win them over. She did everything; she excused every slight, anything to keep her husband from being angry and blaming her for it. He hated all of her friends; there was always something about them he didn't like. The Gentle One would stop calling them, stop meeting them. She was having nightmares, feeling overwhelming fear, and she could not understand where it was coming from. Her husband used every trick in the book to control and manipulate the Gentle One, "No one loves you like I do. No one has ever been this good to you, and no one would put up with you and your family."

Once she took a whole bottle of aspirin, and Allen would not take her to the hospital. He made us lie down on the bathroom floor and drink milk to make us throw up. He said Lina just wanted attention and he wasn't about to give it to us. How that echoed the words of her mother, "She was just doing that for attention. Just ignore her and she will eventually stop." He would not let us leave, and he would not let us call anyone. He wasn't about to put up with the mother's interference, and "for God's sakes don't tell anyone our business." How that haunts us. Her mother would always tell Lina that you don't tell what goes on. It is our family's business and no one else's. Allen was the echo of Lina's mother.

He took her as a sexual object. That's all he wanted. He asked her over and over again if sex hurt ... Oh my God, if he only knew!

Your insides are all messed up. The uterus is out of place, pushed backward, and the ovaries are not where they should be; one is encased in a cyst .We must do surgery, probably a hysterectomy, she was told. She was only 23, too young. Don't tell anyone about our game. The Gentle One could not understand her fear. She could not understand where all those feelings came from. She would close her eyes and see a wall, and the worst nightmare, the most disturbing memory of a pig house.

Lina's husband, Allen, woke up hidden, traumatic memories. He used sex as a weapon to control her as well. He continued telling her constantly, "No one could satisfy you like me." He wanted more and more sex, over and over again, all day. The Gentle One would be so sore and ask him to stop. "NO! I want you to remember what this is like, for no one can satisfy you like I can. No one will ever love you like I do, so you better think about that if you ever think of leaving me." Flashes of pain, flashes of another time, another man, this too would hurt, flashes of a cucumber, of a fist being rammed inside her. Flashes of a doctor going in and seeing what can be salvaged, the doctor asking her if sex hurt. How could she have stood all that pain for so long? Lina wondered if it was supposed to hurt. How could she understand that it should not? The Gentle One could not understand.

We tried to stop her, but she married him anyway. Allen told no one except her family that they were married, and that night he tore her apart for something her sister had said. The Gentle One was confused; was he ashamed of her? He did not tell his children that they were married until one week after. Why? She could not see what we saw. The man was an alcoholic. Even worse, just like her mother, he is a controller, so the Gentle One somehow ended up with someone who had the same traits of both of her parents. She had succeeded in finding a person who could—and almost did—destroy us all.

(Dr. H.): This was written more than a year after Lina had begun therapy. It allowed me to see the cooperation of the Alters, their knowledge and acceptance of treatment, although the Alters, at first, were reluctant to see Lina receiving psychiatric treatment. Lina entered into treatment upon her husband's insistence. For whatever reason he requested treatment for Lina, the fact is that he helped her, and consequently, it also helped others, including him.

I feel I need to talk a little bit about Lina's husband and give some background about him. Around March 1992, Allen was hospitalized with a diagnosis of "severe depression." About two years before that, he started recovering from severe alcoholism. He was hospitalized because of the high risk he had for relapsing into drinking, the poor response he had to antidepressant medication he had been given on an outpatient basis for some time, and the risk of his committing suicide.

I became Allen's attending physician and we developed a good rapport and a positive transference quite rapidly. Once he was discharged from the hospital, I continued providing treatment on an outpatient basis. He was an apathetic person, who had a past history of heavy drinking while in the military. He seemed to manage this without consequences, and received an honorable discharge. He used to say, "The name of the game at that time was to drink, get drunk, and be covered by others."

Once discharged from the military, his drinking increased and got him in a lot of trouble — he was not able to hold a job and was arrested by the police for public intoxication. Finally, after receiving treatment for alcoholism as an inpatient in the hospital, he joined Alcoholics Anonymous. That is what saved his life.

He was a faithful follower of the Twelve Steps recovery process of AA. The first 3 steps are basic: 1. Admitting you are powerless over alcohol. 2. that a Power greater than ourselves can restore us to sanity. 3. that we must turn our will and our lives to the care of God, as we understand him.

I used to call Allen, in a friendly way, "Mr. A.A."

Several times in therapy, Lina's husband used to complain about his marital problems. Marital counseling was not an avenue "because of her," according to him, and "because of him," according to her. I met Lina briefly once before, while Allen was hospitalized. I have a poor recollection of that encounter with her at the hospital. Upon my request, she came to my office with him a couple of times. I wonder today if another reason I took her as my patient was because their marriage was going downhill, and I hoped to help save it. I'm glad I agreed to see her.

CHAPTER THIRTEEN

LINA'S PSYCHIATRIC HOSPITALIZATION.

(Wise One): When Allen went for treatment for his alcoholism, he told Lina she had driven him crazy and it was her fault he was being put away (hospitalized), and she believed him. She was told it was a detoxification center for alcoholism. As she approached the entrance, a voice inside of her told her, "It's not your fault," but she would not listen to that voice. "This is wrong." Allen would not lie to her, would he? The No One could not be contained any longer. We all loved the Gentle One. The No One could not stand by and let her be hurt like that anymore. The No One reacted to Allen's accusations.

Allen was discharged from the hospital. He was walking in front of the house. The No One drove the car up on the sidewalk and tried to kill him. If Allen had not moved, the No One would have run over him instead of hitting a tree. This scared the Gentle One, and she ran on foot to the mother's house. All she could remember was that she had somehow wrecked the car. We knew that the No One would try again. Allen was not safe.

The Gentle One wanted to die, she wanted to go away. Her world was falling apart around her. She could not deal with all the emotions consuming her. The Wall was not holding. Allen was yelling at her. She was attending group therapy, but her female therapist (who was also a recovering alcoholic) was of no use to her and only made her feel worse. The Gentle One was "responsible" for all that was wrong.

(Dr. H.): I knew this therapist very well. She worked in my office for a short time. She did indeed lack an empthetic approach. She tried to be rough and down to earth in her approach, which worked with some patients, but not with Lina.

(Wise One): That group setting ACOA [adult children of alcoholics] did nothing but cause more confusion and increased her feeling that there was something wrong with her. All the Gentle One wanted was to go to the field of wildflowers she saw in a vision in her mind. There was a beautiful lady waiting for her, calling for her and telling her it was all right to come home.

The No One was full of hatred because someone as beautiful as the Gentle One was gone. He blamed Allen, so when Allen came home, the No One was waiting. He knew it would start again, but this time Allen was facing the No One alone. Sure enough, when Allen came home, he started in. The No One would have killed him. He had it planned. He would cut his heart out, and he would have. We had to do something. If he succeeded with his plan, we would all have to answer for it.

The She didn't care. The Bitch was for the No One. It was too much for all of us to contain. The Gentle One was leaving us, the Female Guardian too. Odd feelings of so many years were being released. All the memories were flooding our minds as we fought the

> No One for control. The Male Guardian was like all of us, fighting for some control in the madness, for indeed that was what it was like. Finally, we got the No One locked in the bedroom.
>
> The fight between the Male Guardian and the No One resulted in great destruction in that room. Police intervention followed and partially ended with Lina's admission again into a psychiatric hospital. This happened some time before Allen entered the hospital for inpatient treatment of his depression.

What follows is Lina's typing, and then it switches to the Wise One, with very strong intervention of the No One:

(Lina): Carla is in my mind. She is my granddaughter, my oldest son's little girl. I fought loving her. I fought getting close to her, but somehow she captured my heart. My son and his wife are divorced, and she took Carla to California. It took seven month to find her. I thought that I would die from the pain of that loss. My son has decided to try for custody of Carla, but I feel I'm bad for Carla's case. I have to prove to a court of law that I'll not be harmful to Carla's well-being.

(Dr. H.): Lina's oldest son joined the Navy in California shortly after Lina's second marriage. Then he started drinking and the Navy sent him to a program for alcoholism. I don't know what happened, but he was medically discharged from the Navy. He came back to Kentucky, married, and Carla was born.

Indeed this was anguishing for Lina. At this point, she knew about her MPD problem and was terrified that it could be used in court against her regarding the return of Carla and eventually prevent her from providing care for her. I don't remember how much therapy and time (weeks) we spent on that single issue. I promised her that if I was asked to testify in court, I would testify about what I knew about her — that neither she nor any of the Alters would bring harm to her granddaughter. On the contrary, the No One would provide protection for Carla.

> (Wise One): How this is eating her. Why must this come now? Lina needs love and encouragement. Her new belief in herself is so fragile. We have come so far, and the line is so delicate that it is easily broken. Lina wants to believe that her son is the best for Carla. She knows that the mother loves Carla, but she uses that poor child as a weapon to injure those who anger her. Lina knows this child, but does not know how to answer when Carla asks her, "Why didn't you come to see me? I've been waiting for you." How many times had she as a child not been able to understand? Dr. H. told Lina that she is confusing Carla with herself as a child. Indeed, she remembers the hopelessness she felt as a child.
>
> To make the situation worse, Lina's son is arrested and Carla is screaming in the background, "Mom, you've got to come! Daddy's been arrested! Grandma is going nuts!" We cannot calm Carla down; we must take her out of this. The second son is calling the police to see what bail can be arranged. We take Carla to Lina's sister. Carla fears her mother will come to take her away from her daddy. Carla is screaming, "NO! NO!" So the No One holds Carla; he promises her that he will not allow anybody to take her from him until her daddy is back with her. Carla understands the No One and stops screaming, strange how the No One has that ability. Carla hugs the No One's neck and won't go to anyone else.
>
> The No One rocks her to sleep. Strange how children can sense that he (so ferocious) will not let anyone hurt them.

(Dr. H.): What follows is a strong intervention of the No One. It shows anger and determination, but the rambling does not show a clear picture of what happened that night.

> (No One): What happened? Carla was visiting with her father and for no clear reason, Carla's mother became upset and sent the police to pick up Carla. It seems that Lina's son (Carla's father) was intoxicated and ended up in jail. The oldest son is calling from jail. Bail is $500. It is midnight. His mother wants to get it and post it. She will not get away with it this time! That bitch will have the police come for Carla now — no way will I allow that. She will not get away with it this time. I know her fucking game, and I am the master at playing games. We will get the money together. We won't tell that ass-hole husband of hers. He would just get pissed off anyway. We will cover the loss somehow. The Woman can do without her fucking shopping for a while. We will not allow her to tell Allen about the money.
>
> (Wise One): Lina cannot handle that fight at this time. We will manage to cover the loss. Allen would not understand. Even if he knew everything, could he understand all that Carla is to Lina, another promise broken? Carla's mother does not know, as most adults do not realize, how little a child understands loss. Carla lost her Papaw Pete [?], then she lost her daddy, lost her Nana, her aunt, her dog, Perre and her Grammy [Lina], and she cannot understand why. How well Lina knows that Carla could not possibly fathom the why.
>
> Lina wants the sickness of her family stopped with Carla. Must yet another generation suffer for the sins of the others? Must there always be a circle? We must find an answer, not only for Lina's sake, but for an-

other innocent child that deserves a chance, a childhood.

Lina has not told you that she was a bed wetter. There is so much shame attached to this that is deeply embedded in her. Carla's father was a bed wetter, and so is Carla. Is this not inherited? Just another secret you must not tell.

In the middle of this turmoil, more memories are flowing. It causes difficulty in breathing. She is afraid of the memory that is surfacing. It is dark. It is coming from theWall, triggered by Carla in some way. Lina is alone, her sisters are not there, and mother is again in that place called a hospital, with all those frightening people. Father is gone; seems he is always gone.

The memory is not mine. It is of the Wall. I don't know where the father is. Lina is with Aunt Susie and Uncle Sam, her father's people. The rest is buried. She loved those two people with all her heart. They were her favorites; they always made her feel special. They made her feel loved and wanted. This must be what a family really feels like. Lina felt secure and happy, but as she learned over and over again, this was not for her.

One day her mother returned and Lina screamed, "NO! NO!" They were not there anymore. Grandpa was also gone. What was left?

(Dr. H.): During therapy, the name of Susie and Sam were not mentioned again. Also, I don't recall the name of her Grandfather. Was he Sam? I may be held at fault for not clarifying those and many other facts, but remember that sessions lasted only one and a half hours a week. Although some days we went over that time, it was not enough to cover so many complaints and so much information.

Lina told me that her mother was once kidnapped, raped, beaten, and left for dead. She never told Lina directly about it. Lina found out when the authorities called to notify her mother that the man sent to prison for this was due for release. I met Lina's mother a couple of times and her speech, behavior, and way of dressing was suggestive to me of a person having some sort of an organic mental impairment. Lina told me that her mother had a stroke when she, Lina, was a child. I think this was the time that Lina's father was given permission to return home from Korea, to be with his sick wife.

> (Wise One): Lina tears herself apart. All she wants is to be a Grammie, and even that is not allowed. She asks why. Everyone says to be grateful for the time she had with Carla. They do not understand. It is not HER love for Carla that counts. What is important is that Carla loves HER unconditionally, that Lina can be Lina and still be loved.

CHAPTER FOURTEEN

FACING THE NO ONE. RECOLLECTION OF NO TOE'S SEXUAL ABUSE. THE NO ONE COOPERATES.

(Dr. H.): Lina is learning to accept Carla's move to California. She is learning more about herself and is able to deal with many clear memories that once used to provoke extreme distress, pain, and dissociation. She is accepting reality and more and more she is connecting the past with the present. Her dreams recalling childhood are remembered the next day.

She is having recollections of the No Toe and the many past sexual assaults by him in the Pig House. Now she is able to handle this without the horrible reaction and turmoil of the past and without the need to escape or allow the emerging protection of any Alter.

After two years of therapy, and upon my suggestion, Lina agreed to start watching some videotaped sessions of her therapy. I called that "face to face with herself," meaning face to face with some of the Alters. It was shocking to her to see the No One. She repeated over and over, "How could I be that way?"

It was sad to me to see that face full of anger and hate on the television screen and, at the same time, Lina's face in front of me, so perplexed, inquisitive, and lost.

(Lina): Carla has gone back to California. My life really seems empty. The loneliness crowds into every fiber of my body. I feel the need to be doing something. Maybe I should go back to work. I really need the feeling that work gives me, the satisfaction of accomplishment. I need to fill up the hours. Even taking life hour by hour is becoming hard. I sometimes wish for the old ways, with whole days gone. I feel so insecure now, lost.

I know I wish to put space between me and my mother. The more I'm around her the more agitated I become. I fight the feeling that is growing stronger and stronger every day, that feeling I'm just not comfortable with. It seems as though all my guilty feelings are now slowly melting away and being replaced with hate and anger. I fight the feeling of being trapped and I haven't been able to understand where it is coming from.

I am finally more able to put the blame where the blame really belongs. I was angry at the No Toe.

Now I know why we called him No Toe. I remember seeing his foot with one of his toes missing. I was angry at my mother. I was angry at my father. I was angry at all the people who hurt me and made me feel it was my fault. I was not to blame for what the others in my life had intentionally or unintentionally done. I was/am the victim. Finally, I can see the light— the Wall is falling little by little into pieces. I'm beginning to heal. I do not hear the voices so intensely anymore, and when I do, I know where they are coming from. It is me, part of me. There is no more fight inside of me, no more splitting headaches, no more darkness and confusion with flashes of memory ripping through my mind, and thank God, there is no more time lost, no more escaping from the reality of life. Light is coming through.

I have decided I need to work. I cannot handle a full-time job, but I would like to work part-time. I am racked with fear.

What do I say if I am asked why I haven't been working? What if someone finds out what I am? I am so tired of carrying around the past. I must get beyond that or be trapped forever in a limbo of just surviving. I have learned so much from my Alters. They are forever with me, and we are learning how to live well. I feel better than I have in a long time. I must not let my self-doubt (the She) interfere.

I have been in therapy for two years, and Dr. H. decided that I should meet the others. Dr. H. had videotaped some of my sessions and he had recorded some of the Alters on tape. I heard some of their voices on cassette tapes and read messages that they sent through their talks with Dr. H.

The first reaction I had when I saw the videotapes was shock! Oh God! There on the screen was someone who looked like me and yet didn't. The face, "that face," was so wrong for me. It was the face of someone full of pain; then a change, and from pain, it showed the face of someone full of so much hatred and anger that you could feel it radiating from the screen. There was a female on the screen, but there was no doubt of a male being there. The actions, the sense of masculinity was so strong. Then the voices— they were some of the voices I have heard in my head. I have been hearing them for years as whispers, and now, there they were coming from the screen — from me, and yet, not from me.

From the very beginning, I thought I feared the Alters, but now I realized I feared the memories. I feared the unknown. They had all the keys to unlock Lina Y., and slowly I began to know that person. The No One finally trusted and helped Dr. H. to help me, and I began to understand "them." With therapy, I began to trust (the Alters). Yet I still feared meeting them. The first feeling I had after seeing the Alters was sadness, because they agonized over their very survival. The whole video was a battle fought over a simple contract. They did not mind being videotaped, but when it came to signing a contract that they would not cause any harm to Lina Y., they fought. They would not commit to a year, nor would they commit to a month. Finally, after much agony, they committed to a week. How sad that they could not justify living for more than a week at a time! I grieve, and I can cry for them. I know now that they are a part of me. They have earned the right to continue, for if not for them, I would not be here. They have, each in their own way, been there for me, and now I must be there for them.

(Dr. H.): When we were reviewing these statements, I confronted Lina about the possibility that these words might reflect her resistance to integrate and/or fear of being responsible for her behavior and emotional reactions.

(Lina continued): I'm beginning to remember my dreams. How strange that may sound, but I have never been able to before. I would always say that I had never dreamed, for up until now, I never remembered dreams. Something strange happened, and I can't really tell if it was a dream for sure. It came to me as I was sleeping, but also it was like a memory. The one memory Dr. H. has been working on from the beginning of therapy, the one the Alters told him to ask about. None would claim it as theirs; it always belonged to someone else. Now I know it comes from a four year old who doesn't talk. She just sits with her fingers in her mouth. The Pig House was in my dream.

I'm typing the rest of this from notes that I wrote down when I awoke. I didn't want to take the chance of losing this memory.

There is no face on the man. There is a little girl, no older than four, with blond hair. She is down on the floor. Someone or something is moving up over her back, with whispers of "Let's play a game. I am going to teach you another game." There are boards on the floor, and it hurts the little girl's knees. She is scared. She feels something is not right, but she craves the attention.

My vision is blurred, and I can hardly keep my fingers on the typewriter typing. I'm sweating, and my heart is pumping so hard it hurts. It is hard to breathe. I feel that someone else is here with me.

The little girl has a two-piece short set on. The shorts are blue. Fingers are pulling them down. She feels his touch on her legs as they brush them.

I'm getting goose bumps typing.

A soft cooing voice is saying, "It is all right. It's just a game for the two of us, a secret just between the two of us. You can't tell or we won't play anymore. You wouldn't like that, would you?"

I'm feeling sexually arouse typing, with goose bumps on my legs. My hands are starting to shake, and it's hard to concentrate. I lose the memory at that point.

I had some memory of the Pig House before, but this time I remembered more details. With the help of Dr. H. and Lynny Sue, I can understand the feelings this memory stirs. I'm beginning to understand the She. She took the pain, the guilt, the shame. I understand her "need" to punish and to inflict pain. Someday I may be able to help her finally be free. The No One took the anger caused by the guilt, pain and shame.

So far at this point I have met the Wise One, the She, the Lady, and Lynny Sue. I have gotten to know the Woman, the Guardians, the four year old, the Angry One, and a few of the others, but still I had not dealt with the No One. I truly feared him, for he represented all that was evil to the others.

The Alters feared only two: the She because of her need for punishment and the No One for his power. The No One was from the beginning. He is one of the original Personalities, but he is the last one I met.

(Dr. H.): Before Lina continues describing her "face to face" encounter with the No One, I would like to describe my own emotional reaction when I was made aware of the existence of this Personality within Lina, including my impression after first meeting him, and later on after interacting with him.

The No One may have manifested himself early in the few first sessions of therapy by voicing anger, distrust, and cynicism, with challenging attitude and gestures. But one day, when Lina signed in, my secretary asked me, "Is this Lina? She is so different."

I met her in my office and when she started talking, it was not her voice. It was the tone and pitch of a rough, masculine, angry person. Purposely avoiding using male or female connotation, I asked, "Who are you?"

That question unleashed a furious response, shouting, "BY THIS TIME, YOU SHOULD KNOW WHO THE HELL I AM." Those words were accompanied by a fist-slamming on the top of the desk. He was cursing, denying the existence of God, and blaming society. I felt that the whole office was shaking, the turmoil was so intense, and the shouting was so loud that my wife, who was working in her office, one floor above, came running down and slightly opened the door. She was concerned for my safety. Indeed, it was frightening.

Lina's face changed even more. I remember seeing her eyebrows straighten like a line on top of her eyes. Her eyes went deeper into their sockets and became like dark, glowing pieces of burning charcoal. Her face changed its shape and became triangular. Her mouth was a fine, straight line. Anger was evident and spilling over, and I could see a great potential for destruction from this Personality.

When he (for it was a he) identified himself at the beginning, I asked permission to use the video camera, which we used in past sessions of therapy. He did not object too strongly, and the encounter ended without too much more turmoil. That afternoon I could not find out what triggered this type of reaction. Maybe he was putting on a show in order to let me know the ogre part of this Personality?

After that encounter, every time there was some justification for the No One to surface, the Angry One was the one surfacing to interact with me. Later, I learned that this was not a Personality as such. He was a split from the No One, "created" in order to be able to voice anger without destruction.

In later therapy sessions, the No One would surface, and I confused him with the Angry One. He did that purposely, playing games, as the Wise One told me when I became suspicious. I was alerted not to trust the No One, since he was a master game player and it was possible he was masterminding something. At that moment in addressing myself to the Wise One, I mentioned that we had a previous agreement in which any conversation between myself and an Alter or any split, was to be registered or heard, partially or totally, by the other Alters and Lina, in order to work toward integration and to facilitate Lina being in charge of Lina.

Based on that agreement, and while I was talking to the Wise One, I told them, "I am aware that 'all' you are listening, including you, Mr. No One, and this is not a f——game, using that favorite word of yours, Sir. This is a very serious matter of life or death, and I'm sitting here every week listening to all of your problems trying to help. It is too serious for you to try to plot some game or pull out some unpleasant surprise at this time and at this level of therapy. Either you play with a full deck, or I am out of this. Then all of you, Lina and her husband, mother, sisters, children, and grandchildren are on their own, and I will be free of this anguish every week."

I was angry. I knew I was supposed to keep my cool, to be detached and objective, and that it was unprofessional to use that type of language. I am not trying to justify this outburst of anger, but the effort of unraveling the events of past years along with the interference of actual, valid and disturbing problems in Lina's present life was very frustrating and tiresome. Anyway, it worked!

Lina was going through great turmoil at that time trying to deal with the attitude of her husband, Allen. He was blasting her mother and children, while glorifying his favorite daughter. There were other problems she was trying to solve, plus old, disturbing memories were coming to the surface, provoking further discomfort. I considered her very fragile, and I was worried about a recurrence of her having suicidal thoughts at that time, even though Lina denied that possibility.

Late the next day my phone rang in my home, and a calm but worried male voice asked to speak with me. I was amazed. Here he was, the arrogant, conceited, destructive, insulting No One calling for help. He was saying, "What can *we* do? We are worried for her." (He was talking about Lina).

He sounded very cooperative, concerned, and even polite. We talked for a while and I congratulated him for calling me. "I am glad you called me," I told him. Then I put him in charge (he was anyway), and asked him to consult with the Male Guardian and the Wise One, so they all together could hold the suicidal She at bay and prevent her from acting out until the next morning when I would be talking with "you all and Lina." I also told him to call me that night at any hour, if needed.

The next day, I went to my office early in the morning and I saw Lina. In spite of the crisis the night before, she came alone. She was feeling better and had recovered some control. We talked and when she was leaving the office, I detected a change in her face but I could not recognize it, so I asked, "Who are you?"

"I'm the No One," was the answer.

I told him, "You look different. I don't see your threatening attitude. What is going on? I appreciated your call yesterday. Why the change?"

His answer was, "I can be civil." He smiled, then added, "We will be around if she needs us."

At that moment Lina became Lina again and said, "What a change!"

I was happy that she finally recognized herself with the No One. She saw that he could be a protector, a positive force, and that he was able to communicate in a reasonable manner with me and "the others." I consider this incident a turning point for the better in the therapeutic process.

CHAPTER FIFTEEN

THE DEATH OF LINA'S FATHER

As therapy progressed, Lina was developing strength, security, and freedom. There was still turmoil when she confronted ambivalent feelings, including the love/hate feelings she had toward her father and mother. There was still unresolved grief after the death of her father, and Lina was also facing her memories of her three children. Could she know herself better by knowing the Alters? She continued asking herself, "When and how did that first split happen? Why did it happen to me?"

(Lina): The meeting with the No One, how do I describe all that he brings? He describes himself as my worst nightmare. How do I describe my feelings, my reactions? Dr. H. once asked me what my most profound discovery was. I stated it was the realization that I, as the No One, was capable of murder.

Dr. H. said that anyone, if provoked enough, is capable of violent and irrational behavior. The No One is not only capable of it, he has tried many times to kill. He has plotted to kill, and if not for the intervention and restraining force of the Male Guardian, would have killed many times. This is horrible to me. I see him on the videotapes. I have the face to match the voice in my head. I have a face to identify with the desire for revenge. No wonder I am unable to get angry. There is so much anger and hate in the No One. As I watched that video, I thought, "Oh my God, he is insane!"

Dr. H. said that this was not true. But the looks, the actions terrify me, and yet I have to face the fact that he is a very vital part of me. He has within himself forty-two years of anger, all the hate that Lina Y. could not deal with. How could he be sane? I listen as he brags about watching my father die. I listen as he tells of his plan to destroy my mother. It shocks me to realize he knows my mother better than I. No wonder I am so torn. No wonder I have been unable to deal with the death of my father, the unexplained guilt that won't allow me to even visit his grave. I felt somewhat responsible for his death and to learn that is almost unbearable.

Could I have talked Mom into bringing Dad home? The truth is yes, I could have. Mom begged me to help her decide what to do. My sisters had not been there these last few years watching Dad slowly deteriorate. They had not been there the many times before when the doctors had given up on him, or the many times when the chaplain had been called. Dad begged us to take him home. He said all the doctors wanted to do was experiment on him. Mom and I talked for a long time that day. We even went to make the funeral arrangements together, and she was still asking me to help her decide if the surgery was necessary. I trusted the doctors; they would not say the surgery was necessary if it wasn't. They were aware of his condition. We could not live with ourselves if we brought him home only to watch him suffer even more pain and to watch him slowly die in agony. At least that's what the doctors said. I believed them—or that's what I wanted to believe.

My father was on the operating table from 10 o'clock in the morning until 6 o'clock that night, and he bled to death, because there was "not enough blood supply on hand." There was not any acute infection of the gallbladder; there was no leakage, no emergency to justify the surgery. If not for the hatred the No

One had for my Dad, would I have brought him home? Would my father still be alive? How can I live with this guilt? My life seems to be full of guilt.

(Dr. H.): With that statement, Lina appears to be putting blame for the death of her father onto the doctors and the hospital. Real or not, this is what she felt, and months after therapy ended, I was told that a legal claim was decided in favor of the estate of Lina's father. Lina's mother kept it all.

(Lina): The meeting with the No One brought so many more feelings to the surface. How can a part of me hate so much? Between him and the She, I don't like myself very much. How can I hate them for what I've made of them? They won't leave me like everyone else.

(Dr. H.): Again, here Lina is showing her resistance to be completely independent from the Alters, to be herself for whatever she is. She is still struggling to find out her own identity.

(Lina): Still I can hear my Dad telling me to "let those boys grow up." I did not understand that then. I had them depending on me for everything. "Mom will always love you no matter what you do." I would not be like my parents. My children would never feel rejection. They would know that they were loved. Yet when they needed me the most, where was I?

(Dr. H.): Lina is trying to deal with what she considers abandonment of her three children, and her image of herself as a bad mother.

> (Wise One): She left them just like her mother left her, just like her father left her. She escaped into us. Guilt — how she is wallowing in it. The more she learns, the more she has to face. The ultimate responsibility is hers. Remember those cracks in the Wall, Dr. H.? They are widening. Be careful — they are not mere cracks anymore! Lina looks at her mother and finally sees her as she is. She sees a sick, old woman, and she does not understand how she can be so mean to her. The headache is growing. The depression is

draining her, and there is the She — waiting. Lina's world is gone. Lina is trying to deal with life as it is and how it was. Still she is not prepared for this life.

(Dr. H.): My good Wise One, always worried, always protecting, always trying to guide, alert, warn, and help. I cannot take the merits of the positive outcome of the therapy for myself. The credit should be given to Lina through the Wise One.

(Wise One): I question how much more she should know? So far, the knowledge she has gained has not set her free; it has only increased her depression. She cannot accept that she will never have the family she craves. No matter what she does, no matter what she says or how she acts, nothing will change. Her father is dead; her mother is selfish, mean and controlling; her children are grown and living their own lives. The youngest will have to find his own way; she cannot change what he is, irresponsible, unreliable, without a steady job, drinking. She cannot save him from himself. Her love for him will not keep him from the path life has given him to follow.

The only person she can save is herself. The older son has been living with his grandmother [Lina's mother] after his dismissal from the Navy, and still he continues drinking. He is now in jail. Lina and the No One can do nothing for Carla [the oldest son's daughter].

Lina tears herself apart trying to figure out where to come up with the money for the lawyer. She should know and accept that this is not for her to do. Yet she feels there must be something she can do, and she will not give up. If she does nothing, her guilty feelings will eat her to pieces. If she comes to the rescue of her son again, she takes away his responsibility, keeping him hanging on to her. The problems between her son and his grandmother are theirs, not hers. She

> let them put her in the middle of their problems. She worries about helping her son get a place, but this is not her problem. After all of these years, she finally can tell her mother how she really feels — and then she lets the guilt tear her apart. After all, aren't you supposed to "honor thy mother and thy father"? Shouldn't she be taking care of this sick, old woman? Yet her mother does as she pleases, gets what she wants, and loses nothing.

(Lina): Dr. H. and I were discussing what the Wise One wrote. I'm struck once again with how well they know me and how little I still know about them, but I have gained some understanding. I have learned a lot and have grown stronger.

Yes, I still have doubts. I still have feelings of guilt. I still have fears, but at least now I am not escaping from it. I once told Dr. H. that reality sucks, but given the choice, I chose to deal with it. I still have a lot of growing to do, but now I am not afraid of it. Dr. H. states it best when he says he has given me something I never had before: freedom. Now I must learn to live, for at last I am free to do just that. I have not conquered all there is. I have not gained all the memories or all the secrets from behind the Wall, and I somehow don't believe that what there is still behind the Wall is all that frightening or horrible.

Dr. H. and I spoke of the Wall just last week, and there were no goose bumps, no fast heartbeat. I no longer fear the past, no longer run from the memories. I remember more every day, little things not important to anyone, but me. As Dr. H. once said, "There has to be good memories locked away with the bad," and there are.

CHAPTER SIXTEEN

LINA'S SELF-AWARENESS.

(Lina): Dr. H. asked me to search in my memories and try to find out what feeling — anger, hate, fear, etc. — was the major cause of the original split. As I look back, I try to figure out when that first split happened? Why me? Why did I split?

I have learned from another source that I was a very sensitive child. I am lucky in a way that I can literally see things through a child's eyes. I can honestly say that there are some emotions that a child cannot understand and some feelings that a child cannot endure. As I sat there thinking about the question, I saw the little four year old, and it was as if I felt her thoughts. I felt the answer ever so softly come to mind: rejection. I could feel this child's confusion about not being wanted. I always thought that it was the shame she felt, but I was wrong. It was not shame. When Mom did not believe that child about the "game" she played with the No Toe, it was the ultimate act of rejection in her childish mind. Here was her mother, who was supposed to love and protect her, but instead of comforting her, she just laughed at her story, and the little four year old needed a place where someone would protect her, would comfort and love her and most importantly, not *reject her*.

This is not the complete story of my life. The Alters and I did not include all the events of my life, just some. Now I see that my life, compared to others, was not that terrible. Other people have had much harder lives than mine. This is not really the end of my story. In a way, it is the beginning. Lina Y. is just beginning to live. I am, in a way, much luckier than most people. I now have a much better understanding of myself than most people. I am not alone. Dr. H. promised the Alters that he would never make them go away. Therapy was geared toward integration, not destruction. His hope was to have all of the Alters working together under my control.

(Dr. H.): As I said at the beginning of this book, results or consequences of trauma, emotional or physical, depend not only on the intensity, but also the sensitivity of the receptor. We need to remember that besides the sexual trauma starting so early in her childhood, she had all those religious "rituals" and the turmoil added by her drunk father returning from combat duty, the sickness and hospitalizations of her mother, and all the other situations she could not control.

(Lina): I can just image the No One telling Dr. H., "Hell, no, I won't go," and he hasn't! As I stated before, I am not alone. The Alters and I work together, kind of like a committee. I am the chairman of the board and welcome the guidance of the Wise One.

And where would I be without the help of the Lady? Dr. H. compliments us on how much we have improved. Through the Lady, I have learned poise, the art of makeup, how to dress and how to be a little vain and accept compliments.

(Dr. H.): Lina's husband used to complain about her detachment, coldness, and distance, saying she disliked being touched. By the end of therapy, Lina told me, "Now I have to ask him to put his arms around me because he doesn't initiate any signs of affection."

My advice to her was, "For many years you pushed him away, give him time to adjust to the new wife he is with now."

I continued treating Allen, and at the same time I could monitor the progression of Lina at home with Allen's feedback. He was anguishing because Lina wanted to fly to California to visit Carla. He was repeating over and over, "She will not come back. She will disappear like before. This trip to California is her excuse to leave me."

(Lina): From the Bitch, I have learned to be assertive, and now I stand up for myself. I have gained confidence with her help. Veronica, the worker, kept all my skills. She retained the knowledge that enables me to work, even if it is part-time work. How can I thank the Female Guardian for her gentleness, her caring? The Male Guardian with the Female Guardian protected the Core. Even the No One has given me so much, and I have learned so much from him. He fought all my battles to protect me from all the bad. How simple it sounds now!

(Dr. H.): Regarding Veronica, it seems that she came into being when Lina was in her very late twenties or very early thirties. When Lina decided to finish her education and started working, her boss asked her why she was signing some memos with the initials V. A. and she didn't know why. Lina described Veronica as the soft-spoken, reliable, efficient, competent, hard-working part of her. Even today, Lina doesn't know why or where the name Veronica came from. She cannot identify her with any person or remembered event. I presume that Veronica could be a split.

Veronica, as well as the She, the Bitch, the Woman, the Lady, the Shell and even Rowdy, are integral parts of the Core, who came into being in Lina's adolescent and adult life. What I don't know, and I do not think it is important to know, is which are the basic Alters or Personalities, and which are the splits. Those mentioned above were functional Personalities, performing tasks and daily living activities.

(Lina): There are so many things that I have not included in this story. Some are important, but I don't think it is necessary to include all that there was. I have just written a small part of what they endured for me so that all could survive. I can see them in my head. Not a picture, but in my mind I see them talking to me. They still argue a lot, but now I can stop their chatter. Now I'm in control, but I respect them enough to listen to their warnings, their fears and their ideas, and every now and then, I let them out.

The children still like to play, the Lady loves to shop, the No One loves to drive my husband's car with the radio blaring rock music. The difference now is that I'm in control and aware of what they are doing, so the Wise One and I know when to stop them. The Guardians are still there and I hope they always will be.

(Dr. H.): As I have said so many times at the beginning of this book, I did not have any previous experience treating a patient like Lina, so I do not have parameters to compare and judge the success or failure of my work with her. But I was watching the results and outcome of the treatment and it was positive.

When Lina wrote — "the Wise One knows when to stop them" — referring to the No One and the Guardian, the two most powerful Personalities within Lina, it seems that they were loosing ground against the humble, soft-spoken Wise One Personality. What a drastic change this was. How and when did it happen?

When therapy ended one day and Lina was leaving my office, my secretary asked her if she were driving the beautiful, new car parked in our parking lot. The answer came with a grave tone of voice, "No, she is not driving, I am. She doesn't know how to drive cars with stick shifts."

When Lina stated, "Now I'm in control. . . I respect them. . . now and then I let them out," what did she mean by that? Can we call this "Integration," and was my therapy successful?

I was then facing my retirement from active medical practice. I needed to let my active patients know about my plans. I started giving referrals to my patients to see other physicians for continuation of treatment.

Lina's husband accepted seeing somebody else, but not Lina. "When you retire, I will go to no one else. I will be your last patient," she said.

Deep in my heart, I wish I could have provided or continued therapy for Lina for a few more months, in order to have a better understanding of everything, but I was tired. Therapy was ended and I retired from active practice a few months later. Lina was indeed my last patient. Today she and her husband are my friends.

(Lina): The problems are still there. My mother will always be my mother. What is different now is how I feel. I don't feel guilty when I tell her no, when I don't give into her demands. I still don't visit my Dad's grave much, but not out of guilt. I feel that my Dad is not in the grave, but forever locked in my heart. Most importantly, I can love them both, for now I know them for who they really are, just human beings like me, like you, not perfect, but a product of what life gave them.

With regard to my children, I do not feel guilty for what I did or didn't do when they were growing up. I have learned to accept that I did the best I could. Now the only thing I can do for them is let them live their own lives and let them solve their own problems so they can grow.

Carla will be forever in my heart, and no one can take her away from me there. I call her, and I can hear the laughter in her voice. Yes, it still hurts that I don't see her as much as I would like.

My husband and I are still together. I know he has had a rough time. My memory brings me unpleasant events from my past when I am with him, but I now can say, "I'm sorry, it is not you."

I have said all I have to say. I hope that my story can help someone else, not just a "multiple" like myself, but maybe someone out there wondering if they should give up or try again. I guess what I'm trying to say is just don't ever give up. As long as there is a little spark of life, there's hope.

Dr. H. asked the Alters if they believed in God, and the answer was, "Who is God?". So he proposed an idea, "Maybe, whoever He is, He is the one who is there for us to find." I'd like to think that. I only ask, what took Him so long to show me the way to acceptance and happiness, the way to freedom.

EPILOGUE

On December 13, 1995, I saw Lina's husband, and he was still having problems accepting the "new" Lina, unsure if she was going to maintain so much change and improvement. He could not adjust to what he called a challenging attitude. Lina felt that the Bitch had helped her to be assertive so that she was able to talk to her husband and express her own ideas and opinions. It seems that he was still afraid that she would disappear again and not come back, even though Lina had not gone away from home since therapy started three years before.

At one session, he told me that Lina had needed to go to the emergency room because of stomach problems. He told me that one of her sisters was badly bitten by a dog, and that Lina was very upset. He also told me that she was still confronting unresolved problems with her mother and her three grown children.

I saw Lina that same afternoon and I was concerned because this was going to be my last formal session of therapy, since I was closing my office practice in one week. I was positively impressed by the way Lina was handling her problems. This time she was the one helping me to help her husband.

I continued communicating with Lina. I called her several times to find out how she and her husband were doing. A couple of times, my wife and I took her and her husband out for lunch. People who knew her from the time that she started therapy, and who saw her a couple of years after, were amazed to see such a drastic change in her, regarding the way she was dressing, taking care of herself, and her personality. She makes me feel good about myself and I feel really good about her

She continued improving more in areas of self-esteem and ego-strength and had a better attitude, which allowed her to endure the stress of daily living, with on and off acuteness of problems.

Lina was very receptive to my idea of writing her history and making it available in a book for lay people.

The results of her therapy were worth the initial effort invested. She told me that I was a wonderful doctor, a good psychiatrist, and a nice human being.

I shared the following story with her:

"Once upon a time, a very difficult patient told me while we were engaged in therapy, 'You are full of it.' I looked in his eyes and told him, 'You are right.' He was surprised that I agreed with his statement. Then I added, 'When I'm with my wife and my family, I am full of happiness and love. When I play piano, I am full of melody. When I go to church, I feel the proximity of God.' 'So,' I told Lina, 'I'm reflecting what you are, and you are a good person. Therapy was not easy, but you put forth your best effort. I tried the best I could as well, and I'm glad we did it.'"

Fifteen months after the last session of formal therapy—I say "formal," because in every phone call I had with her and her husband, I tried to convey a positive attitude to both—I asked Lina to type her impressions and feelings so they could be included in this book.

She sent the page which follows.

AFTERWARD

LIFE WITHOUT DR. H.

Dr. H. asked me to write an Afterward. How has my life been since Dr. H.? I have started the answer to this question at least three times. It really isn't as simple as it sounds.

At first it was hard. I depended on Dr. H. to be there picking up the pieces and putting them together for so long. I was afraid of being on my own, but I was quickly reminded that I was not alone. The Old Ones will always be with me.

I'm better able to cope with my life, for it is not a fairy tale where everyone lives happily ever after. Life is not like that. It has its good with its bad.

As I glance back over my writings, I find that as childish as it sounds, I expected that once I was "fixed," then everything would be great. My family would suddenly see how together I was and they would be fixed, too. I would finally have the loving family that for so long the children created for themselves, but that is not the way it is.

The family is made up of complex human beings each with a life all their own. I have grieved over the problems that have manifested themselves in my children, for I know I played a part in them. The only thing I am able to do is to love them and accept them and go on with my life.

I find I am once again at a crossroad in my life. In many ways I am content with my life. I now see my grandchildren regularly. (My oldest son has a new baby boy). I still see my mother, and most of the time, I can deal with her. She has remarried, and I like my stepfather and believe he is good for Mom.

I still suffer headaches, but not like before. Now I find when there is a decision to be made and I put off making it, the Alters let me know. I still suffer from depression, but again, not like before. The She is still with me, but I do not fear her as much. I found out that the She is more of a reminder that I must deal with certain feelings and not let them bottle up.

I spoke with Dr. H. the other day, and he asked me about the Wall, if anymore of the old memories locked away have come out. I told him I thought so, but I wasn't sure. I can still see the Wall, but the old fears are not there anymore. There are many cracks in the Wall now, and yes, there are some stones missing. The Alters seem to know that I can cope with the past. I can recall things from my childhood that I never could before. Not all of it is bad; there was a lot of good, too. As I stated before, I am basically content with my life. I still have a lot of health problems to deal with, and I still have my husband, but life with Allen is another unfinished chapter.

Well, I hope this helps someone.

FINAL COMMENTS

A few months after therapy started, I noticed that Lina was developing some insight, a capacity to understand what was going on within herself. The Alters were coming to the surface, sometimes on their own, and other times upon my request or encouragement. I then started encouraging Lina to start writing whatever she remembered of her life or dreams or anything that could help put memories and feelings together.

In this book, I do not pretend to explain every symptom or any of the many manifestations or characteristics of what is known in the text books about "Personality Disorder."

So, this book consists of the Lina's writing and reports, but while she was writing, "others" were taking over off and on, to either clarify some statements or to continue describing the events in Lina's life about which she did not have any memory or recollection. Most of the writing was done by one Personality who manifested himself very early in therapy who called himself the Wise One. Thanks to his cooperation and help, therapy ended with positive results.

Another powerful Personality named the No One manifested himself a few times by writing or explaining what was written. He also managed to handwrite several notes to me which were brought by Lina. A few weeks before the end of the treatment, he called me on the telephone and asked for advice and help.

From that time on, he stopped fighting and quarreling, and became a very useful ally in the therapeutic process. When the No One showed a positive attitude, I felt more confident that the potential for Lina's destruction was fading away.

Many questions remain unanswered. One of those is the question of how people in similar conditions like this are responsible for their actions. Was Lina responsible for the destructiveness of the No One? How valid is the term "transient psychosis," which has been used so often in court to justify outbursts of deviant behavior by a person that was previously described as "normal"?

Perhaps the most interesting question of all came at the end of therapy, when Lina finally was in charge of her life. Can we safely say that integration of those Personalities was accomplished, when Lina still affirms the presence of some Alters? According to some experts, the answer to this question is yes, since Lina was, and still is, in charge of her life.

I do consider Lina's life and treatment different from any other cases reported previously.

Ten years after therapy concluded, Lina is living a stable life with the normal ups and downs of daily living.

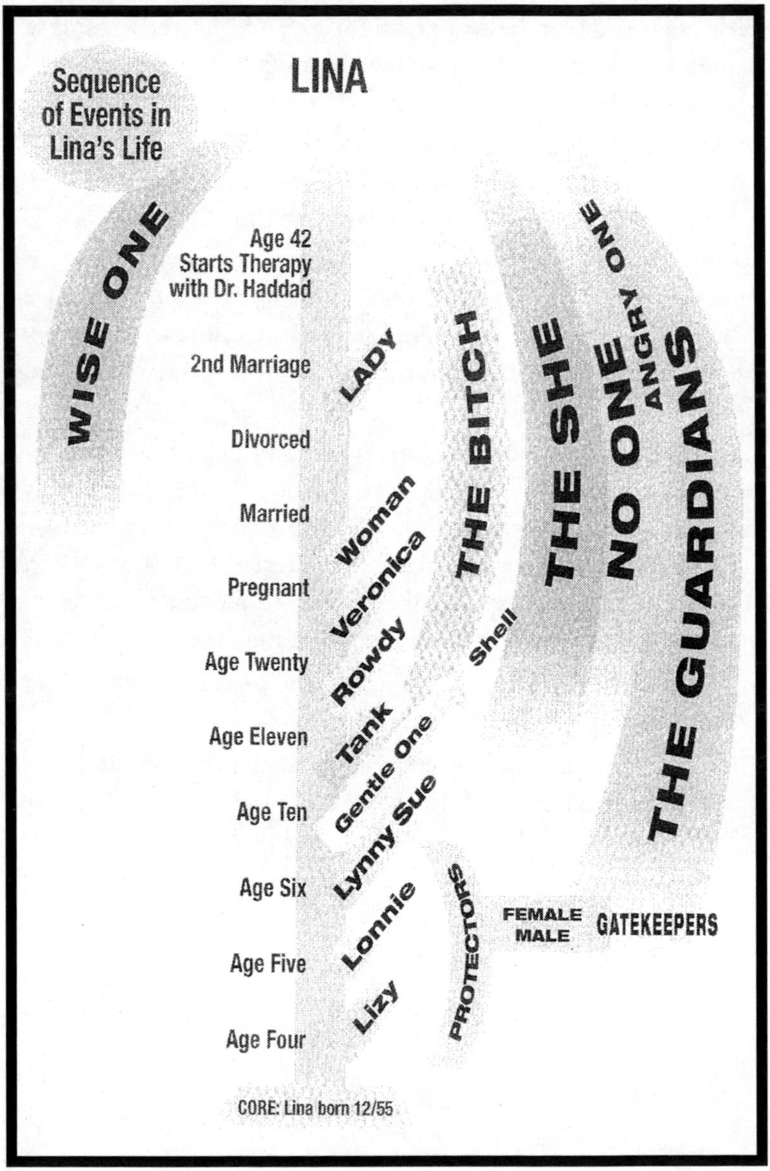

Sequence of Events in Lina's Life

LINA

WISE ONE

Age 42
Starts Therapy with Dr. Haddad

2nd Marriage

Divorced

Married

Pregnant

Age Twenty

Age Eleven

Age Ten

Age Six

Age Five

Age Four

CORE: Lina born 12/55

LADY

Woman

Veronica

Rowdy

Tank

Gentle One

Lynny Sue

Lonnie

Lizy

THE BITCH

Shell

PROTECTORS

THE SHE

NO ONE

ANGRY ONE

THE GUARDIANS

FEMALE
MALE

GATEKEEPERS